SQUEEZE
— the —
MOMENT

Karen O'Connor

SQUEEZE

—the—

MOMENT

31 Days to a
More Joyful Heart

WATERBROOK
PRESS

SQUEEZE THE MOMENT
PUBLISHED BY WATERBROOK PRESS
5446 North Academy Boulevard, Suite 200
Colorado Springs, Colorado 80918
A division of Random House, Inc.

Scripture taken from the Holy Bible, New International Version®. NIV®
Copyright © 1973, 1978, 1984 by International Bible Society. Used by
permission of Zondervan Publishing House. All rights reserved.
Scripture marked (NASB) is taken from the New American Standard Bible®
© Copyright The Lockman Foundation 1960, 1962, 1963, 1968, 1971,
1972, 1973, 1975, 1977. Used by permission.

The names, professions, ages, appearances and other identifying details
of the people whose stories are told in this book have been changed to
protect their anonymity, unless they have granted permission to the
author or the publisher to do otherwise.

ISBN 1-57856-222-8

Library of Congress Cataloging-in-Publication Data
O'Connor, Karen, 1938-
    Squeeze the moment : 31 days to a more joyful heart / Karen O'Connor. — 1st ed.
        p.   cm.
    Includes bibliographical references.
    ISBN 1-57856-222-8
    1. Christian life. I. Title.
BV4501.2.O323   1999
242'.2.0323—dc21   99-14486
                                                            CIP

Printed in the United States of America
1999— First Edition

10 9 8 7 6 5 4 3 2 1

FOR JUNE

with love and joy

CONTENTS

Part 1: Waking Up to Life

Part 2: Thirty-One Days to Joy

Part 3: Continuing the Journey

Part 4: Personal Pages

PART ONE

Waking Up to Life

INTRODUCTION

Cultivating Joy

W hile I was leafing through an issue of *Reader's Digest* some years ago, an article entitled "Lessons from Aunt Grace" caught my attention. The author, Nardi Reeder Campion, described a time in her life when she felt depressed, even hopeless, until one day she discovered an old diary kept by an aunt forty years earlier.

Frail, poor, and alone, Aunt Grace had depended on relatives for her care. "I know I must be cheerful," she wrote, "living in this large family upon whom I am dependent, yet gloom haunts me.... Clearly my situation is not going to change; therefore, *I* shall have to change."[1]

According to her diary entry, Aunt Grace resolved to do six things each day in order to change her perspective and make her little corner of the world a happier place. These six things included doing something for someone else, doing something for herself, doing something she didn't want to do that needed doing, doing a physical exercise, doing a mental exercise, and saying an original prayer that included counting her blessings.

The rest of the article describes how these six precepts helped change Ms. Campion's life just as they had changed her Aunt Grace's life decades before. "Can life be lived by a formula?" asks Campion. "All I know is that since I started to live by those six precepts, I've become more involved with others and, hence, less buried in myself."[2] She learned to follow her aunt's motto: "Bloom where you are planted."

I was heartened by what I read. If such actions worked for these women, I thought, maybe they could work for me. I was facing some tough times myself. Relocating to a new city and being separated from some of my family, good friends, and familiar surroundings, I needed more than just encouraging words. At the same time, I didn't want to cram another set of rules into my life. I had had enough "should" systems, self-help seminars, and feel-better workshops. What I wanted was more freedom, more joy, more surprises.

I was eager to become more alert to life by performing kind acts for others—in the moment—just as Aunt Grace had done. I also wanted to be kinder to myself—giving in to that urge for a nap in the middle of the afternoon or taking my deck chair to the nearby park and just sitting for an hour under a big old tree. If I gave myself a little treat now and then, I reasoned, I'd probably feel more like doing those things that needed doing, like balancing my checkbook, having the tires on my car rotated, or being nice to someone who annoyed me.

I decided to take a few of Aunt Grace's precepts and make them my own—customize them for my daily life. Three of them were already in place. I was exercising every day, and I had plenty of mental stimulation in my work as a writer, so doing something physical and mental didn't catch my attention the way the other principles did. And I had been keeping track of my blessings for years. In fact, that routine had prompted me to write the book *Basket of Blessings: 31 Days to a More Grateful Heart.*[3]

So I chose to focus on the first three precepts: doing something for others, doing something for myself, and doing something I didn't want to do that needed doing. And then I added a fourth: looking for joy in unlikely places. I didn't practice them in any particular order, and I didn't do each one every day. I considered them reminders rather than rules, there to help me not only seize the moment but *squeeze* it as Aunt Grace and her niece had done. Those women not only practiced making the most of their circumstances, but they also actively pursued a sense of purpose and joy. They embraced their present moments and milked them for the richness they contained.

The more I began to participate in life instead of simply to pass through it, the more joy I felt. I woke up in the morning eager to squeeze each moment—whether walking along the beach, working on a book, praying with a friend, talking with my husband, attending a meeting, or playing with my grandchildren. I was becoming alert to life! Joy began to well up inside me. The sunsets were more beautiful to me than ever before. The birds in the tree outside our bedroom window seemed to sing just for me. Tasks I once dreaded—cleaning closets, purging files, returning phone calls—were suddenly easier because I was doing them with a heart of joy. Sometimes they were even pleasant!

Then one day something remarkable occurred, something I never would have anticipated. Yet as I look back now, I know it was meant as another reminder to squeeze the moment. Very early that winter morning I walked toward the laundry room in our apartment building, feeling terrible because I had forgotten to transfer my clothes from the washer to the dryer the evening before. In our large building of many tenants and few washers and dryers, each family had only two hours a week to do laundry. So my memory lapse would cause some other tenant great inconvenience if I didn't quickly get in and out before the person with the 6:00 A.M. slot arrived. I wanted to make sure the machines were empty and ready to use and the folding space was wiped clean.

Too late! As I pushed open the door, there sat Laverne, my neighbor down the hall. She was leafing through a magazine as the washers and dryers pounded rhythmically beside her. "Good morning," she said brightly.

"Good morning," I replied. "I'm so sorry…last night I got caught up in…and I forgot to…"

She finished my sentence for me. "Forgot to put your clothes in the dryer?"

"Right," I said, too embarrassed to look her in the eye. I walked toward the folding tables, expecting to find my wet, rumpled clothing in a heap. But instead I saw two piles of socks and shirts and towels and underwear—mine and my husband's—dried and neatly folded.

"Laverne…did you…" I gestured to the clothing.

"I did," she said, smiling. "I got here early today, so why not?"

"You didn't have to do that," I said. "I feel bad that you had to handle our clothes at all. But then you dried and folded them too!"

Laverne looked at me, her eyes shining with kindness. "I didn't mind," she said. "Isn't that what we're here for? To help each other?"

Slowly I rolled her words over in my mind. *Isn't that what we're here for? To help each other?* Wow! And I thought I was going to do *her* a favor.

Here was a woman who knew how to *squeeze* the moment. She sure taught me a thing or two that morning. And it didn't have anything to do with laundry!

I hugged her tight, piled my clothes in my basket, and went upstairs feeling more joyful than I had in weeks. Fortunately for me, Laverne didn't abide by the '80s recovery slogan, "Don't do for others what they can do for themselves." In fact, I doubt she even knew that doing for others had earned a bad rap, that it could be construed as codependent behavior or, worse yet, as a way to avoid dealing with her own problems. No, Laverne didn't worry about any of that. She just did what came naturally to her. She helped a neighbor. She recognized an opportunity to be generous and kind, and she gave herself to it. She *squeezed* the moment and brought joy into an unlikely place: a dim laundry room before dawn. I can't help but think some of that joy spilled over onto her as well as me.

You, too, can invite more joy into your life each day. I have written this book to encourage and inspire you to do just that—first by becoming more alert to life so you can quickly recognize moments of opportunity as Aunt Grace did, and second by embracing and squeezing those moments for the joy they contain.

[1] Nardi Reeder Campion, "Lessons from Aunt Grace," *Reader's Digest*, July 1984, 92.
[2] Campion, "Lessons from Aunt Grace," 94.
[3] Karen O'Connor, *Basket of Blessings: 31 Days to a More Grateful Heart* (Colorado Springs, Colo.: WaterBrook Press, 1998).

HOW TO USE THIS BOOK

The purpose of these daily pages is to ignite in you a desire to respond immediately to opportunities God brings your way, to be spontaneous, to move in the Spirit, to see a need and to act on it, to do good without constraint, even to experiment. Think of Aunt Grace. She was challenged to live her last years dependent on relatives, the perfect setup for a pity party. Instead she responded creatively to life, one day at a time. I like to imagine that soon after she made up her mind her precepts became such a part of her life she didn't have to think about them. She just did them. I hope that will happen for you, too, and that, as a result, joy will flow naturally.

The thirty-one daily readings illustrate the four precepts I mentioned in the introduction: *doing something for others, doing something for myself, doing something I don't want to do (that needs doing!), and being open to giving and receiving joy in unlikely or unexpected places.* All the stories in this book are true, although some of the names and identifying details have been changed to protect identities. Think of these stories as fire starters, bits and pieces of paper and wood that when ignited will grow into a bonfire of joy and satisfaction.

After you've read the day's story, ponder the scriptures that follow in the "Words to Reflect On" section.
Many of the days include a reading from Psalms because
its main author, King David, is such a good role model
for turning to praise and joy, regardless of the circumstances in life.

Then use the "Looking Within, Living It Out" questions to stimulate your thinking about how the day's
reading relates to your life, how you can squeeze the
moment with greater abandon and thereby experience
joy spontaneously.

Next, use the "Prayer Starter" to open a time of praising God and petitioning him to guide you as you live a
more joy-filled life.

In the last section, "Holding On to the Joy," note
the times you experienced unanticipated joy through
your own giving or through someone giving to you.
Maybe something in the day's story will remind you of an
event in your life when you took hold of the moment
and squeezed it. Or perhaps you missed an opportunity
and now see what you might have done differently. All
insights are worthwhile, each one moving you forward
on your journey toward more joy.

At the end of thirty-one days, celebrate! Read over
your journal entries, and look back on the moments of
that month. Did you squeeze from them every last drop
of sweetness and satisfaction? Did you let some opportu-

nities pass you by? How did other people respond to you? How did you feel? What events and experiences increased your spontaneity and enlivened you with joy?

Consider going through the book again the following month, this time inviting your spouse, roommate, friend, or child to participate with you. The daily reading can lead to a satisfying and edifying discussion. If you live alone, make these occasions intensely personal. Guard this time between you and the Lord, and don't allow anything to distract you.

There is no *right* way to approach this topic or incorporate these precepts into your life, so make this *your* journey. Use this book for support and inspiration as you begin to live more spontaneously and joyfully. If no one else in your life shares your enthusiasm, don't be discouraged. Maybe God is calling you to be an example in others' lives.

People who focus on joy, who look at life through its lens, and who express joy in all their dealings and relationships have a more satisfying life. I pray that you, too, will be motivated to look at your life in a fresh way and to *squeeze* your moments—the happy ones, the tragic ones, the predictable and unexpected ones—for all they're worth. May you find the treasure each moment contains.

PART TWO

Thirty-One
Days to Joy

DAY ONE

Entering Someone Else's World

The first gift I received from my new husband was a rod and reel," said Marie. "That was over forty years ago." Next she received a shotgun for hunting. Not very romantic, she admits, but Marie later realized that both the gun and the pole gave her a unique opportunity to enter her husband's world, to learn more about him, to spend more time with him.

While other men left their wives or girlfriends behind to pursue their outdoor hobbies, Marie's husband, Norm, wanted her to share these experiences with him. "Other items were added to these initial gifts," Marie said. "His-and-her fishing jackets and caps, licenses with plastic envelopes, and safety pins to fasten them to the jackets. Certainly a new fashion statement for me," she quipped.

"We cast our lines into farm ponds and cool mountain streams in West Virginia and Kentucky, from ocean piers in Florida and Georgia, and around the oil rigs in Lake Pontchartrain in New Orleans. I never became great at fishing—though I did land a trophy fish once—but I became an expert at sharing my husband's life."

Marie reflected on those days, then added, "My husband has given me many romantic gifts over the years, but none were more meaningful than my rod and reel."

Today Norm is quite ill and no longer active. But Marie looks back at their long marriage with great joy because she made the most of the opportunities they had. She cherishes the memories of those weekends spent hunting and fishing together.

In today's world, feminists would have a field day with such a story. "Why didn't he enter *her* world?" they might ask. "Isn't this just one more example of how men oppress and manipulate women?" Could be for some. But not for Marie. She *chose* her man, and she *chose* how to live her life with him. Being *with* her husband was more important to her than anything else. She happily admits her marriage was different from many of her friends'. She also says it was wonderful, and she has no regrets.

I'm inspired by Marie's lifelong commitment to do something for someone else by entering her husband's world with determination and devotion for over forty years. Each of us can do something similar with our mates, our children, our friends, our family, even strangers.

My husband and I have been given numerous opportunities to do something for someone else, and when we take advantage of them, our lives are shaped and enriched in new ways. When we let such opportunities slip away and forget to squeeze the moment, we are the poorer for it.

For six years we hosted foreign students in our home. We made some of our dearest friends during that time, people young enough to be our children and close enough to feel like family. We could have provided just a bed and breakfast, dinner, and TV, but we made a point of spending time with these kids, and we were blessed for having done so. I count those years among the richest of my life. When I think about hovering over a map of Switzerland with Kurt, lingering over dinner in conversation with Florian from Austria, walking along the shore with Christina from Italy, and helping Marco from West Germany with his English homework, I am filled with joyful memories. The students' enthusiasm for these new experiences helped me focus on the moment and squeeze it! We made the most of the time we had together.

Rodger Whistler and Walt Bailey have entered the world of newborns. They are part of the "Cuddler Program" at the UCSD (University of California, San Diego) Hospital. Some of the wee ones swaddled in hospital receiving blankets aren't much bigger than Rodger's and Walt's large hands. As Rodger gazes into the dark eyes of baby Kaylin and plants a little kiss on her tiny pink finger, he jokes in a soft voice, "I've roasted chickens bigger than this." The fifty-eight-year-old building inspector declared in a recent newspaper interview, "The night I come here [to the hospital] is the best night of my entire week."[1]

"This is my weekly reward," added eighty-three-year-old Bailey.

These two men are not only seizing an opportunity for joy, they are *squeezing* it. What joys are waiting right around the corner in your life? Run ahead and discover what opportunity awaits you.

WORDS TO REFLECT ON

Do not withhold good from those who deserve it,
when it is in your power to act.

PROVERBS 3:27

Dear children, let us not love with words or tongue but with actions and in truth.

1 JOHN 3:18

Give, and it will be given to you. A good measure, pressed down, shaken together and running over, will be poured into your lap. For with the measure you use, it will be measured to you.

LUKE 6:38

LOOKING WITHIN, LIVING IT OUT

- Whose world could you enter today? Someone right in your own household perhaps?

- In what specific ways might you enter someone else's world? Perhaps with a smile, a handshake, a listening ear?
- Has anyone brought joy into your world? Who was it? What did he or she do?
- Today, be alert to life so you will be ready to bring joy into someone else's world or to receive his or her gift of joy in yours.

PRAYER STARTER

Dear Lord, today I will be spontaneous as I interact with people at home, at work, in the community. I want to be ready on a moment's notice to enter the world of at least one other person. I know you'll be there with me. Give me your eyes that I might see each person as you see him or her. Help me to seize the moment, to squeeze it, and to receive the joy that flows when I am open to your leading and your will.

HOLDING ON TO THE JOY

Jot down something you've done for someone else that required you to enter his or her world. How did you squeeze the moment?

[1] Barbara Fitzsimmons, "Male Bonding: Cuddling Attracts Three Men and Lots of Babies," *San Diego Union-Tribune*, 7 October 1997, Lifestyle, E-1.

DAY TWO

Giving Up Our Right to Be Right

I could be wrong." "I'm not sure." "Maybe I made a mistake." "That's a point I hadn't considered before." Imagine the profound sense of well-being we could have if we were willing to give away our right to be right. What a weight off our shoulders!

This selfless act might be overlooked by others. It might go unacknowledged for a time. It might even look a little crazy. But that would be just fine. Giving up being right does not require that anyone else approve or even notice. Do it for yourself even more than for another! If it's at the top of your list of things you really don't want to do, you can be pretty certain it needs to be done. So do it! And watch what happens.

Even when we're absolutely sure we know what to do, how to do it, and where to do it, we could be wrong. Someone else might know more or have a better idea, a more interesting perspective, or a more workable plan. Consider how it might feel to bow to that, to give up your certainty, to declare your vulnerability, to allow someone else to be right.

Does it really matter, for example, which way you and your spouse drive to the airport, as long as you get there safely before the plane takes off?

Is it essential to load the pantry or refrigerator or dishwasher your way? Or could your child or mate or friend do it differently and it still work?

Must your way of running a meeting, filing a report, balancing a bank account, or teaching a class be the only way? Or could you release these tasks to others and in the process learn something new?

Answer this question honestly: Are you a control freak? Sometimes I am. I've faced each one of these circumstances in my life, and I admit that when I held on to my position, I felt tense and irritable. When I released my grip, however, suddenly the how and why didn't matter as long as the goal was reached or the task was completed. And you know what? Each time I let go, I was relieved. It actually felt good to let someone else take over. I had no idea that right behind the door marked "control" was a flood of joy waiting to be released!

I smile just thinking about it.

"I gave up my right to be right," said my friend Paul, "when we lost our daughter to cancer. Until that time I knew it all. I was the resident expert on driving, cleaning, cooking, handling money, taking care of the yard. But I wasn't even close to knowing how to handle Lisa's death.

"Suddenly I didn't care about being right. I didn't care about anything except getting through the pain. And that's where my wife came in. She had strengths I needed. She had information that I had never taken seriously before. Being right didn't matter anymore. I gave it up. Now it's easy to say, 'I don't know. What do you think?' or 'I could be wrong' because I really could be."

Paul said his experience was similar to mine. The more he let go, the more relaxed he felt, and the more willing he became for life to unfold naturally. He began smiling. He was more playful. "We have joy in our home once again," he said.

Giving up your rights could be as simple as giving up the right of way. Why not try it for a day? If you pull up to a four-way stop and someone else edges out when it's your turn, give away your right. Smile and wave the driver on. If you're standing in line at the bank, post office, or grocery store, and someone behind you has fewer items than you, even though it's *your* turn next and you're in a hurry too, step aside and let that person move ahead.

Today give up your right to be right—even if it's something you don't want to do. See what happens! You might be surprised at how serene and truly joyful you can feel.

WORDS TO REFLECT ON

The LORD is my light and my salvation—
whom shall I fear?
The LORD is the stronghold of my life—
of whom shall I be afraid?

PSALM 27:1

Do not be afraid; you will not suffer shame.
Do not fear disgrace; you will not be humiliated.

ISAIAH 54:4

Command them to do good, to be rich in good deeds, and to be
generous and willing to share. In this way they will lay up trea-
sure for themselves as a firm foundation for the coming age, so
that they may take hold of the life that is truly life.

1 TIMOTHY 6:18-19

LOOKING WITHIN, LIVING IT OUT

• How might you experience joy in giving up your right
  to be right?
• Think about a time you forced your viewpoint on others because you couldn't bear to be wrong. What were
  the consequences?
• Consider a time you were convinced you were right

21

only to discover later that you were wrong. How did you feel? What did you do about it?

• Today be open to giving up control so you can be receptive to joy.

PRAYER STARTER

Dear God, my face is red! I confess I like to be in charge. Even when I procrastinate, I am exercising a form of control. I don't like to let other people have the last word, win the race, be first in line, or come up with a better idea than mine. *I want to be right.* But I also notice that when I impose my point of view on others or elbow my way through life, I feel alone and ashamed. I lose the joy that results from depending on you and taking direction from you. Lord, restore my soul, refresh my spirit, renew my mind so that I can disengage from situations that separate me from the joy you freely give.

HOLDING ON TO THE JOY

Jot down your thoughts about a time you could have given up your right to be right but didn't. Reflect on how that situation might have turned out differently if you had. How could you have squeezed the moment and discovered its joy?

DAY THREE

Noticing Signs of Hope

Christmas is a sign of hope, bright with the promise of God among us in his Son, Jesus Christ. We exchange gifts, sing carols, decorate our homes and hearths, and gather with family and friends to celebrate this day of days. It is a time to rejoice and reflect, to feel encouraged and exhorted, to pray and praise. What great opportunities we have during this season to squeeze the moment as we give to and receive from one another.

For some, however, Christmas is a season of dichotomy, filled with reminders of things present and past that challenge us to lean on God. Sometimes we are so caught up in our pain and worry that we forget God sent his only Son to meet us right there in the midst of difficulty. We need help finding our way back to the hope he brought into the world that night in Bethlehem.

Lynn had such an experience several years ago on a cold day the week before Christmas. "In the still of winter, death's darkness enveloped me," she said. "Birdless, leafless trees and my father's incurable kidney disease testified to death's stark reality. I was consumed with worry, unable to experience God's joy and to trust his provision for my father."

One day after saying good-bye to her dad in front of the dialysis center where she drove him for treatments three times a week, Lynn said she was struck by the poignancy of a naked little tree, bravely defying winter's onslaught. "It was a painful reminder of my father's frailty and failing health," she added.

"Then suddenly, as if dropped from heaven, a beautiful, red-breasted robin settled on one of the tree branches, adorning it like a ruby-colored Christmas ornament. In the bleak chill of winter, I was amazed to see this little harbinger of spring, a sign of hope. I praised God for this unexpected gift of joy and for the precious gift of time—another day with my father."

Lynn said she also stopped to thank the Lord for his most generous gift of all, his Son born into this world of sin. "He would die for humankind on a naked tree," she said, "and rise victoriously from a cold tomb, defying death and ushering in new life—the springtime of eternity."

Lynn said that at that moment she stopped worrying. "God flooded my heart with joy and with the knowledge that no matter what happened to Daddy on earth, he would live eternally with the Lord."

If you're passing through a dark night at this time, look up. Notice the signs of hope God has placed in front of you, if you will but see. Notice that the blacker the sky is the brighter the moon and stars are. Stand firm. Do not waver. Allow God to use the backdrop of this dark night to display the glow of his countenance. He is faithful. After every night, daylight comes.

WORDS TO REFLECT ON

Why are you downcast, O my soul?
  Why so disturbed within me?
Put your hope in God,
  for I will yet praise him,
  my Savior and my God.

PSALM 42:5-6

Satisfy us in the morning with your unfailing love,
  that we may sing for joy and be glad all our days.

PSALM 90:14

Be joyful in hope, patient in affliction, faithful in prayer.

ROMANS 12:12

LOOKING WITHIN, LIVING IT OUT

• What are some of the signs of hope you have received in the past?
• How are hope and joy related?

- How has God used a dark night in your life to minister hope?
- Ask the Lord to rekindle the joy of hope in your heart.

PRAYER STARTER

O Lord, you have taught me that my hope is in you and that if I remain close to you and obey your commands my joy will be complete. Yet I often hold on to my hurts as a child holds on to a favorite toy. I want to change that today. I release to you all obstacles that I have erected or accepted from others, and I place my hope in you alone. Open my eyes to notice the signs of hope you place before me today.

HOLDING ON TO THE JOY

Choose one of the scriptures from page 25 to meditate on. Then write about how it applies to your life today.

DAY FOUR

Becoming a Stream in the Desert

My father-in-law, Charlie, loved to tell the story of how a friend came to his rescue on Black Tuesday in 1929. Charlie had planned to withdraw some cash from his bank account the day before, but he got busy doing chores and didn't make it before closing time. "I'll go first thing in the morning," he told his wife, Ada. But the next day was too late. The stock market had crashed. Banks closed—for good.

Later that day Charlie met his friend Miles Butler in the street. Charlie told Miles what had happened. On the spot Miles reached into his pants pocket and pulled out $700 in cash. "It's all I've got in the world," he said, "but you've got nothing. Here, half is yours," he continued, peeling off $350. "And you don't owe me a penny."

Some sixty years later a Ms. Butler stepped up to the customer-service counter at Nordstrom department store to pay her bill. My husband, Charles, who works there, commented on her last name. "Butler. I haven't heard that name in years. Miles Butler was my dad's best friend in Kentucky," Charles said, making small talk as he processed the woman's paperwork. Ms. Butler appeared interested. Charles proceeded to tell her the story of his dad, Charlie, and his friend Miles on that fateful day.

Two days later Ms. Butler returned to the store with a message for my husband, who was off that day. "James Miles Butler was my paternal grandfather's brother," her note read.

What an amazing discovery! A moment of spontaneous generosity between two men who are now gone gave birth to another moment of joy between two of their family members who had a chance meeting sixty years later.

Like my father-in-law, millions of people are caught at times in the desert of life, limping across the burning sand without resources, without hope. Maybe you've been there. I have. When we meet men and women in this place, it's an opportunity to be a refreshing stream for them. God will show you what and where and how much to do. Even a small stream makes a big difference to a person who is materially and emotionally dry.

Your stream, like Miles's, may continue watering others for decades to come, even after you're gone. Your stream can refresh the children at a homeless shelter when you read to them, tutor them, or help serve meals to their desperate families. Your stream can restore hope to a bedridden person who has given up on life and on

God. Your stream can revive a single parent who is parched to the bone from the stress of rearing young children alone. Take her kids for an hour or so. Go to the park or out for ice cream.

The Harrises helped a refugee family from Kurdistan get settled in the United States by contributing to a pool of housekeeping items. "It was our pleasure to give them cookware, drinking glasses, bedding, and towels," said Pat, "but more important, to welcome them to our community and enjoy their friendship."

On the first Sunday of each month the ushers at our church take a special collection for families in various parts of the world who have a serious need. One Sunday we raised over $1,000 for a Cuban family who had been displaced during an uprising in their homeland. For the average American family this would hardly make a dent, but for this family it could mean the difference between life and death.

Combine your stream with others', and you can flood an entire desert: a crisis center for unwed mothers, an orphanage in Mexico, a nursing home, a children's hospital—all need the water of love and service and practical help you can provide.

At times your stream may seem to disappear in the vast sea of sand around you, and you may feel your own spirit run dry. "Why me, Lord?" you may ask. "There is so little I can do." He is quick to respond and faithful to

29

lead. "I will instruct you," says the Lord, "and teach you in the way you should go; I will counsel you and watch over you" (Psalm 32:8). It would be difficult not to experience an abiding joy in such a moment as this!

WORDS TO REFLECT ON

Blessed is he who has regard for the weak;
the LORD delivers him in times of trouble.

PSALM 41:1

He who is kind to the poor lends to the LORD,
and he will reward him for what he has done.

PROVERBS 19:17

Be devoted to one another in brotherly love. Honor one
another above yourselves.

ROMANS 12:10

LOOKING WITHIN, LIVING IT OUT

• For whom could you be a stream today? In what way?
• What desert experiences have you had where kindness could have made all the difference?
• Sometimes being a stream might involve sacrifice. How are joy and sacrifice related?

- Today look for opportunities to "water" someone who is weary and parched; then note the joy you feel as you squeeze the moment.

PRAYER STARTER

Faithful God, you are the Living Water in my life, and I thank you that because I know you, I will never thirst again. What joy I feel in that assurance! So many people need what only you can provide. Sometimes they don't even know what they need because they hurt so much. Today I pray that I will be open to those around me, sensitive to their needs, and willing to be a stream of hope in their desert places.

HOLDING ON TO THE JOY

Stop now and consider the desert experiences you've had. It may feel overwhelming just to think of what you've been through. Write down your thoughts and feelings. Then note how God has sent refreshing currents into your barren places.

DAY FIVE

Simplifying with Delight

One afternoon my husband and I decided to do something we had been putting off for a long time: We cleaned out the clutter in our apartment. We knew it needed doing, so we made it a gift to one another and then promised to reward ourselves with a good meal at our favorite Greek restaurant.

I started on the closets, piling unused clothing, books, and kitchenware into bags. Nearby, Charles tackled boxes of old files and yellowing paper.

"I feel as if we're coming down to where we ought to be—to a life of simplicity and order," I said.

"I agree," said Charles. "Let's keep at it till we're finished."

Simplicity, we discovered along the way, is—quite simply—freedom from useless accessories, ornamentation, show, pretense, and clutter. Simplicity need not be austerity or asceticism, which renounces the things of the world. Rather, simplicity puts those things in proper perspective. We're free to *be* and to enjoy our lives, without making a show of it one way or the other.

Practicing simplicity involves prudence. I discovered this the hard way as I tripped over umpteen pairs of shoes I hadn't worn in years! Take it from me: Think twice before buying what you want. Buy what you need! Do we really need ten pairs of shoes, for example, or two irons and two can openers, or a television in every room? Can we enjoy our clothing for several seasons rather than adopting every fashion trend that comes along? Are we willing to live in a modest dwelling that is affordable and comfortable, rather than a showplace that drains our earnings each month?

Simplifying may also inspire us to clear out the material and emotional clutter in our lives—from old magazines to people who drain our energy and time, from used clothing to negative emotions.

Do we really need to subscribe to every publication that interests us? Must we accept every invitation we receive? Could we share resources such as a lawn mower or a snow blower with neighbors? Are we willing to let go of beliefs and biases that keep us stuck in relationships that dominate or derail us?

How liberating it can be to use something without owning it. Wouldn't it be lovely to be free of dusting items we don't need, fixing things that continue to break, replacing equipment that wears out? And wouldn't it be refreshing to meet new people, participate in a new activity, visit a new place?

Living a simpler life also has given me the time and desire to develop a love of nature. The Lord teaches us that creation is good and is to be enjoyed. "And God saw all that He had made, and behold, it was very good" (Genesis 1:31, NASB). I enjoy hiking, walking among the flowers, collecting shells at the beach, sleeping under the stars in the desert. During a recent walk in the country with one of my daughters, I was blessed by her comment, "A few minutes out here is enough to show me again how few material things I really need." The simple life is contagious!

The discipline of simplicity can also be applied to our inner life. I noticed, for example, that I could clear out some of the spiritual and mental clutter I was plagued with: trying to read six books at once—a morning devotional, an evening devotional, a woman's study Bible, a biography, a classic, even a Christian novel! Who was I trying to impress? I now focus on one book at a time in addition to my Bible, and I'm actually reading them through and enjoying them.

For a while I felt compelled to sign up for every seminar and every Bible study that was offered at my church. I was spending so much time attending classes and doing homework that I had lost my joy and my spontaneity. I stepped back and realized that God is more interested in my relationship with him than in how many notches I acquire on the belt of Christian education!

Talking about the simple life is easy; actually *living* it can present a challenge. Like the rich young ruler in the gospel of Matthew, we have lofty intentions until we are called to put them into practice. On the other hand, if we go to the opposite extreme and renounce all possessions as evil, we become legalistic, taking pride in turning away from the things of the world.

My husband and I haven't mastered the art of simplicity by any means, but we now stop and consider carefully before we add to our possessions or take on more activities. We've made a practice of purchasing things for practicality rather than prestige, giving things away regularly, sometimes things we're not finished with, even things we treasure.

We continue to discover that simplicity brings us down to where we ought to be, so God can lift us up to where he wants us to be. Simplifying produces joy because there is less between us and the awareness of his presence.

WORDS TO REFLECT ON

This is the one I esteem:
> *he who is humble and contrite in spirit,*
> *and trembles at my word.*

ISAIAH 66:2

He guides the humble in what is right
and teaches them his way.

PSALM 25:9

For the grace of God that brings salvation has appeared to all
men. It teaches us to say "No" to ungodliness and worldly pas-
sions, and to live self-controlled, upright and godly lives.

TITUS 2:11-12

LOOKING WITHIN, LIVING IT OUT

- In what ways do clutter and chaos stand between you and squeezing the moment?
- How are joy and simplicity related?
- What would you need to give up in order to have a simpler life?
- Do one thing today to simplify your life. Then notice the joy it brings.

PRAYER STARTER

Dear Lord, please help me today to let go of the physical and emotional clutter in my life that stands between you and me. I see how stacks of paper, disorganized cabinets and closets, piles of unused clothing, difficult people, unresolved emotions, and hurts and misunderstandings from the past keep me from experiencing the joy of your presence. I stay stuck in the world instead of reaching for the peace of your Spirit. I want to change that today, dear God. I trust you to give me the grace to take the first step.

Holding On to the Joy

Write down the most significant physical, emotional, and spiritual items that clutter your life. Then spend a few moments listing ways to simplify those areas. Notice how you feel when you finish writing.

DAY SIX

Responding to the Spirit's Prompting

*M*y wind chimes saved me the other day," my friend Bonnie wrote in a note from her home in Hawaii. "I was feeling frantic in getting ready for my move to California. I'm overwhelmed with all the preparations. It's going to take a major leap, physically and mentally."

Bonnie painted a word picture of the state of her apartment as she contemplated what to do next. "Here I am sitting in the middle of my living room floor submerged in stacks of important papers, piles of mismatched clothing, mementos strewn here and there, and a line of beloved photos standing in a far corner. Everywhere I look," she wrote, "there seems to be a sign flashing, 'Pick me. I'm the most important!'"

Within seconds, she said, a gentle breeze rustled through the palm trees outside her window. "I glanced up in time to see a small, almost imperceptible movement of the wind chimes hanging from an overlay on my roof." The tinkling sound was loud and pronounced, as if calling Bonnie to attention.

Decisions about what to take, what to leave, what to

give away before moving were suddenly less critical than they had been just moments before. The most important decision right then, she realized, was to respond to the gentle promptings of God's Spirit: to relax, to listen, to be kind to herself.

"Suddenly I felt better," Bonnie said. "My mood shifted. The soft breeze, the sound of the chimes, and the rustling leaves filled up that space in me where discord had been." She felt peaceful about going back to her tasks, knowing she would be guided from within.

Lisa's story is another example of what can occur when we respond to God's promptings. "It was a sunny Saturday," she said, "my only day off for the week. I finished my errands and was ready for a relaxing afternoon. While driving home, I passed a house on a corner in my neighborhood. An elderly lady was pushing a lawn mower, while another lady, who appeared to be disabled, watched from the front porch."

Lisa took one look at the tall grass, the uneven shape of the yard, and the powerless mower and felt the urge to stop and offer help. "But I had my day planned, so I drove home," she said. "However, I continued to feel God's nudge to give these neighbors a hand. It wouldn't go away. So I decided to go back."

Lisa approached the woman pushing the lawn mower and offered her a hand. But the lady was very vocal about not needing any assistance. She would do just fine on her own, thank you very much! The woman on the porch, however, called out, "God bless you. You are so sweet to offer."

Lisa said she went away with a joy she had rarely known. "Not because they said no and, therefore, I had the rest of the day to myself," she explained. "And not even because I had offered to help a stranger. My joy came from listening to God's prompting—and obeying."

These stories are typical of how doing something for yourself—being kind when you're under stress, listening for God's leading when you're self-absorbed—can ennoble your own life and spill into the lives of others.

Each day is filled with opportunities, choices, decisions—invitations to squeeze the moment. Most come from the outside. Not often enough do we pause, notice, listen, and only then take action. We need to free ourselves from the tyranny of the urgent so we can obey the promptings of the Spirit. Then, whether he uses tinkling wind chimes or a struggling neighbor to get our attention, we will be ready to respond with joy.

WORDS TO REFLECT ON

For this God is our God for ever and ever;
   he will be our guide even to the end.

PSALM 48:14

For day after day they seek me out;

they seem eager to know my ways,

as if they were a nation that does what is right

and has not forsaken the commands of its God.

They ask me for just decisions

and seem eager for God to come near them.

ISAIAH 58:2

The one who received the seed that fell on rocky places is the
man who hears the word and at once receives it with joy.

MATTHEW 13:20

LOOKING WITHIN, LIVING IT OUT

- What does being kind to yourself mean to you?
- How can obeying God be a gift to yourself?
- What has God used in your life to guide you this week? Did you pay attention and follow his direction?
- Be open today to responding to the promptings of the Spirit.

PRAYER STARTER

Dear God, today I want to be open to the direction of your Holy Spirit. I confess that I am in too much of a hurry. I seem to measure the quality of my life by the quantity of my work! I want to give up this stressful practice. I know your Spirit is within me, urging, guiding, leading, and protecting. Help me today, O Lord, to pause, notice, and listen before I act. And then may I follow your lead with confidence and joy.

HOLDING ON TO THE JOY

Jot down some of the Holy Spirit's promptings in your life. How have you responded?

DAY SEVEN

Appreciating a Second Chance

Day after day I walked along the concrete walkway that leads from our condominium unit to the stairway. And each day I was annoyed by the sight of a bedraggled, overgrown plant hanging over the edge of the walkway above, down to the second floor where I live. "Why don't they *do* something about that thing?" I often thought. "It's an awful sight, and it's half-dead anyway. Why not prune it? The plant would thrive if this lonely tentacle weren't sucking energy from the main shoot."

I had it all figured out...if only my neighbors would ask for my advice! But they didn't. I complained to my husband about it, and he said emphatically, "Leave it alone. It's their property."

"But it's unsightly," I argued.

"Don't look at it," he countered.

I should have listened. But I didn't.

One day I could no longer resist the urge to clip, clip! So I did. I reached over the railing with my pruning shears and snapped them shut around this ailing limb. It dropped into my free hand, and I sent it down the trash chute! I felt better—almost heroic. I had put this poor thing out of its misery.

I went on with my day, working at my desk, returning phone calls, responding to mail. In the late afternoon I went out to the post office. When I arrived home, I ran up the stairs but was suddenly stopped by the sound overhead of a woman crying. Then I heard the soothing words of another woman, who appeared to be sympathizing with the first one. I looked up, and there stood Lois, my neighbor on the third floor. Our neighbor Jean stood alongside, arm around Lois, as the two commiserated about the plant that had been mutilated by some uncaring person below.

My stomach went into such a knot I can't describe it. I don't remember ever feeling so humiliated and anxious. I felt like a criminal. My heart pounded so fast I could hardly talk. But I knew what I had to do. I had to confess.

I set down the mail on the spot and ran upstairs, breathless. "Lois," I said, "I'm the culprit. I'm the one who cut your plant. I'm so sorry. I should have asked first. Charles told me to leave it alone. It was your property. But I thought it would be okay to prune it a little since it was hanging over the railing all the way down to the second floor...and..."

I couldn't stop. I was mortified, embarrassed, apologetic, and defensive—all at the same time!

Lois listened with eyes wide in disbelief. And Jean didn't know what to say. I stopped. And Lois spoke. She told me how she had worked so hard to get that little plant going. Finally when it was thriving, someone just cut it off. She couldn't imagine why anyone would be so cruel.

Of course she was right. It was cruel, even though I didn't see it that way at the time. I was so caught up in my opinion of what looks good that I took action regardless of how it might affect another person.

I was off to a poor start on a day when I had wanted to do something nice and unexpected for another person! Unexpected, yes. Nice, well…

I apologized profusely, wanting Lois to understand that I wasn't motivated by spite (though I wasn't sure at that point). I had just wanted to tidy it up a bit!

She thanked me for being honest, dried her eyes, and we parted.

The rest of the day was pure misery for me—not so much because of the plant. I knew it would keep growing. I hadn't destroyed it. But I had hurt a neighbor. Someone I like. A person who lives close by.

I couldn't let it rest. I prayed about what to do. Then I ran downstairs, jumped in the car, and drove directly to the local nursery. I spent some time selecting a beautiful, thriving, flowering plant that looked similar to the one I had cut. I bought it and wrote a card, acknowledging my fault once again and asking for Lois's forgiveness.

Within moments of leaving the gift at her doorstep, I received a call. Lois accepted my apology and thanked me for such a thoughtful gesture.

At the end of the day I realized that doing something for someone else that day had turned out differently than I expected, but still, it had turned out. I made things right when I had been wrong, and in turn, my neighbor did something for me. She gave me the gift of a second chance.

That night I lay in bed reflecting on the great value of such a gift, so grateful for all the second chances God gives me each day.

WORDS TO REFLECT ON

But from everlasting to everlasting
    the LORD's love is with those who fear him,
    and his righteousness with their children's children—
with those who keep his covenant
    and remember to obey his precepts.

PSALM 103:17-18

Yet if you devote your heart to him
    and stretch out your hands to him,

if you put away the sin that is in your hand
    and allow no evil to dwell in your tent,
then you will lift up your face without shame;
    you will stand firm and without fear.

JOB 11:13-15

Therefore, as God's chosen people, holy and dearly loved, clothe yourselves with compassion, kindness, humility, gentleness and patience. Bear with each other and forgive whatever grievances you may have against one another. Forgive as the Lord forgave you. And over all these virtues put on love, which binds them all together in perfect unity.

COLOSSIANS 3:12-14

LOOKING WITHIN, LIVING IT OUT

- Who in your life needs a second chance?
- How might your mercy bring joy to that person and to you?
- In what areas of your life has God given you the joy of a second chance?
- Today pray for guidance about extending a second chance to someone so you both can experience God's love and mercy.

PRAYER STARTER

O God of second chances, you never shut me out. There is always a candle in the window, a key to the door of your throne room, a place at your banquet table for me when I have strayed. Today, dear Lord, show me the people in my life who want a second chance from me. Fill me with the joy that overflows when I give more than asked for and offer more than deserved.

HOLDING ON TO THE JOY

Consider a time when you were aware of God's giving you a second chance through someone else. Write out the experience, and comment on how it changed you.

DAY EIGHT

Turning Darkness into Light

If perfect earthly sight were offered to me tomorrow, I would not accept it," wrote Fanny Crosby, one of the most inspiring and well-known women of the nineteenth century. Preacher, hymn writer, influencer, Fanny said that by living in darkness (from the age of six weeks) she was "better prepared to sing [God's] praises and incite others so to do."[1] If she had been distracted by all the beautiful things around her, Fanny later claimed, she could not have written the thousands of hymns that were meant to be sung all over the world.

What most people would have considered a tragedy Fanny Crosby saw as an opportunity. She found joy in unexpected places, and she turned darkness into light as she traveled from city to city, praying and preaching the gospel. She became a model for women and for people with physical challenges, long before either group was widely recognized.

Fanny's life was one of deep trust and joy in the Lord, regardless of what was going on around her. As she served others, she experienced his provision in every way she needed. Perhaps her life could be best summed up in the words of one of her most famous hymns: "To God be the glory, great things He hath done, so loved He the world that He gave us His Son."

As Fanny Crosby's life was drawing to a close in the United States, another great writer was beginning to achieve recognition for her writing while living in China, where she had been born of missionary parents. But it did not come without cost. Pearl S. Buck, winner of the Nobel Prize for Literature in 1938 for her novel *The Good Earth*, had undergone, just eleven years before, one of the most devastating experiences of her life.

While living in Nanjing with her husband, John, an agriculture teacher, and their two daughters, Pearl wrote her first novel in the attic of their modest home. She finished the book early in 1927 but never had a chance to submit it for publication. In the spring of that year a great uprising against China's warlords took place. This revolt was carried out by combined forces of soldiers loyal to China's two major political parties, the Nationalists and the Communists.

The revolutionary armies invaded Nanjing on March 27, intending to take over the city. As the troops advanced, the Bucks were forced to flee from their home. A servant whom Pearl had helped many times before allowed the family to hide in her little mud hut. But later that evening they were discovered by the invading soldiers, who took the Bucks to the university, where other white prisoners were being kept. For a time Pearl thought everyone was going to die. Finally the Chinese generals agreed to release non-Chinese and allowed them to board an American destroyer.

The Bucks arrived in Shanghai with only the clothes on their backs. Pearl's recently finished novel had been destroyed by the invading soldiers. And looters had taken her books and her beautiful green coat.

Yet Pearl claimed she felt a sudden sense of freedom and joy. "I knew that anything material can be destroyed," she later wrote. "On the other hand, people were more than ever important and human relationships more valuable."[2]

Pearl Buck, Fanny Crosby, and many thousands of people throughout history have found light in the dark and difficult places—sometimes by choice, often through challenging circumstances. We can too!

So often we take for granted the joyful and peaceful moments that are part of each day—until we are faced with experiences that threaten or destroy things we hold most dear. Then we realize what we have lost. But when we face our losses, as Fanny Crosby and Pearl Buck did, we are humbled by the sudden presence of God himself—often when least expected. He is right there, leading the way out of darkness and into the light.

WORDS TO REFLECT ON

You, O LORD, keep my lamp burning;
  my God turns my darkness into light.
With your help I can advance against a troop;
  with my God I can scale a wall.

PSALM 18:28-29

The LORD is good,
  a refuge in times of trouble.
He cares for those who trust in him.

NAHUM 1:7

The path of the righteous is like the first gleam of dawn,
  shining ever brighter till the full light of day.

PROVERBS 4:18

LOOKING WITHIN, LIVING IT OUT

- In what specific ways has God led you out of darkness and into the light?
- How have the dark periods in your life influenced your relationship with the Lord?
- How might you comfort someone who is struggling in the dark?
- Choose one of God's promises just quoted, and meditate on how it applies to your life.

Prayer Starter

Faithful Lord, when it's dark and I feel lost, it's difficult to squeeze the moment. It's challenging even to imagine that I'll ever feel joyful again. But I have experienced your presence when I have lost loved ones to death. I've learned more about gratitude during financial stress than at any other time. I've experienced unexpected joy even during an acute illness. I learned during those times how present you are to me; I know now that I am never alone. You are the light that overcomes all darkness. May I take refuge in you.

Holding On to the Joy

Describe in detail one episode in your life when God led you from darkness into light and what that meant to you.

[1] John Woodbridge, ed., *More Than Conquerors* (Chicago, Ill.: Moody Bible Institute of Chicago, 1992), 108.

[2] Karen O'Connor, *Contributions of Women: Literature* (Minneapolis: Dillon Press, Inc., 1984), 62.

DAY NINE

Stepping Out with Gladness

I'll never forget my tenth birthday. My father left work early and picked me up from school, his new black leather ice skates slung over his broad shoulders and my new white ones in his hand. "We're going down to the pond to skate," he said, "just the two of us. It's my birthday present to you."

The mere thought of having my father all to myself brought tears to my eyes. He worked long hours in those days, and it was rare that he took time off for leisure.

I waved good-bye to my friends, and off my dad and I went to the nearby pond, now frozen hard after a week of subfreezing temperatures. I wrapped a wool scarf around my neck, pulled my stocking cap over my long brown hair, and donned my mittens. Then hand in hand, Dad and I skated all afternoon. Whenever I hit a bump or felt scared, he was there, stretching out his hand to hold me up and to guide me through the maze of skaters whizzing by.

As the sun began to set, we piled into our old tan car, our noses red and our cheeks cold. As we drove home, our hearts were bursting with warmth—for one another, for the fun we had had, for the celebration of my tenth birthday. I skated many times after that, but never did it mean as much to me as that special day alone with Dad.

A few months ago one of my granddaughters unexpectedly invited me to *her* tenth birthday party. The afternoon would include lunch at a favorite restaurant and indoor ice skating at a local rink.

I said yes to lunch but no to skating. "I haven't skated in forty-five years!" I told Sarah. "I'd be scared to go out on the ice after such a long time. But I'll have fun watching you and your friends from the bench."

For the rest of the week, however, I wrestled with my decision. "You're not a sit-on-the-sidelines kind of grandma!" I told myself. "You're a tree-climbing, mountain-hiking, tag-playing grandmother." I wanted to skate. But I was afraid. Back and forth I went. Yes, one day. No, the next. The Saturday morning of the party I made up my mind. I would get out on the ice and see what happened!

When it was time to skate, I gulped hard, held on to the guardrail the first time around, then took a deep breath and stepped out into the whirl of skaters. "If only Dad could be with me," I whispered. I blinked at the tears that stung my eyes. What a memory today would have evoked for both of us!

"O Lord," I prayed, "help me do this. It's a chance to overcome my fear and resistance and to participate fully in Sarah's birthday." Then suddenly I realized I was skating—really skating. The more confident I felt, the faster I went, round and around, excited by this newfound freedom. My heavenly Father was upholding me, just as my earthly father had done so many years before. Fear vanished as the truth of God's promise in Isaiah swept across my mind and encouraged my heart: "For I am the LORD, your God, who takes hold of your right hand and says to you, Do not fear; I will help you" (Isaiah 41:13).

I felt renewed in that moment. If God would uphold me in a simple thing like ice skating, surely he would be there for all the big challenges in my life. As I glided around the rink, I promised the Lord and myself that from that point on I would step out without hesitation—and squeeze each moment at home, at work, and in my community, knowing that my heavenly Father is right there holding my hand.

WORDS TO REFLECT ON

May those who delight in my vindication
shout for joy and gladness;
may they always say, "The LORD be exalted,
who delights in the well-being of his servant."

PSALM 35:27

Gladness and joy will overtake them,

    and sorrow and sighing will flee away.

ISAIAH 51:11

Is anyone happy? Let him sing songs of praise.

JAMES 5:13

LOOKING WITHIN, LIVING IT OUT

- What are you "dying" to try, even though you're afraid?
- What can you do to overcome your resistance?
- How might doing something you don't want to do strengthen you and bring you unexpected joy?
- Do at least one thing this week that you don't want to do (but that needs to be done). Notice how you feel as a result.

PRAYER STARTER

Dear Lord, today I pray for the courage to take bold, new steps in my life, to overcome fear, and to try things I have resisted. I want to step up to experiences and activities that challenge me, strengthen me, and cause me to lean on you for guidance and protection. I commit to trying something new—something I don't want to do but know I should do—so I can let go of the thoughts and beliefs that have frightened or intimidated me for too long. As

I step out with childlike gladness, I know you will fill me with joy.

HOLDING ON TO THE JOY

Think of a time when you challenged yourself to try something new. Maybe you gave a speech when you were terrified, prepared a holiday dinner for thirty people, skated with your children, asked for a raise or a promotion. Describe one of those experiences, and note how you felt as a result of stepping out in faith. How do you feel about it today?

DAY TEN

Connecting with Loved Ones

It was a beastly hot day," said Diana, "and I had taken my seven-year-old granddaughter and my nine-year-old grandson to the YMCA swim center to cool off. We cavorted in the pool until we were exhausted."

As Diana drove home, she realized that once again they had had fun together but hadn't had any meaningful conversation. "They were step-siblings, so there was often rivalry and dissension between them. I prayed for a chance somehow to encourage a better relationship. I knew that when we reached their house it would be too late. The toddlers in their family would be too much of a distraction."

At that moment Diana remembered a book sitting on the front seat of the car. "I pulled over to the side of the road," she said, "and stopped under a tree."

"Why are we stopping?" both grandchildren asked at the same time.

"I have a story I'd like to read you."

Diana knew just the one she wanted to read. It was about a boy who saved his little sister from a charging bull. It wasn't a long story, but the message was clear: Take care of those you love! The children loved the story, and they liked the surprise of stopping unexpectedly. As Diana drove home, it also became clear from their behavior that they had gotten the message of what she read!

Susan also wanted to connect with her family, especially since many members were far-flung across the United States and Canada. So in the fall of 1993, she took a break from her job as a concierge at a San Diego resort and from her coursework at San Diego State University.

"I was feeling burned out," she said. "I decided to get away from all my concerns and fulfill a longstanding dream. I began planning what I called my 'Friends and Family Tour,' which would take me around the perimeter of the United States and through parts of Canada."

The trip would include planes, trains, automobiles, and buses. On a student's budget, that was a tall order. "I needed some creative financing," said Susan, which she managed by arranging to sleep on couches in spare rooms in the homes of family and friends. "It was a time to connect with others," said Susan, "and to explore this vastly diverse and beautiful country."

In all, Susan visited forty-seven cities over five months—including walking in the French Quarter in New Orleans, biking in Cape Cod, hiking on the

Appalachian Trail in New Hampshire, and camping in Yosemite. "Planning and participating in this adventure was one of the best things I've ever done. I allowed myself a reprieve from the daily grind, and I gained a whole new perspective on my life," she added.

Susan said she returned seven thousand dollars poorer, yet millions richer in life experiences. "No price can be placed on the value I gained," she added. "Catching up with the lives of so many people I care about was a priceless gift that I gave myself. I had just the right balance of solitude and shared moments."

When Susan returned, she was surprised with the happy news that the job she'd quit at the resort was once again available. The person who had taken her position had resigned a couple of weeks earlier.

When we give to others, we give to ourselves as well, and when we do something special for ourselves, it spills into the lives of those we love. Pick up the phone today, or jot a note to someone you'd like to reconnect with. Arrange a get-together. Then follow through.

WORDS TO REFLECT ON

I am the LORD your God,

who brought you up out of Egypt.

Open wide your mouth and I will fill it.

PSALM 81:10

Be devoted to one another in brotherly love. Honor one another above yourselves.

ROMANS 12:10

May the God who gives endurance and encouragement give you a spirit of unity among yourselves as you follow Christ Jesus, so that with one heart and mouth you may glorify the God and Father of our Lord Jesus Christ.

ROMANS 15:5-6

LOOKING WITHIN, LIVING IT OUT

- What do you most enjoy about your relationships?
- What do your family and friends most enjoy about you?
- Which of your relationships could benefit from a fresh connection?
- Today think of at least one thing you can do to deepen your relationship with a friend or a member of your family.

PRAYER STARTER

Dear Lord, so often I have waited for my family and friends to reach out to me. I'm hurt if days and weeks go by without some time together. I can sit back and seethe with expectation, or I can call them, telling each one that I miss and love him or her. A shiver of joy runs through me just thinking about the possibilities. Help me, God, to squeeze these moments today.

HOLDING ON TO THE JOY

Describe what you'd like to do on a visit with one of your loved ones. Write down a plan, then contact that person.

DAY ELEVEN

Experiencing Joy in Tough Times

Margaret was startled awake one Sunday morning by the piercing ring of the phone. As she reached for the receiver, she had no idea what lay ahead.

"Becky's in the hospital," her son-in-law said. "She ran a high fever on Saturday with severe stomach cramps, diarrhea, and vomiting, and now she can't breathe on her own. The doctors don't know what's wrong, They'll do a CAT scan today."

Margaret's mind leaped to conclusions. What if her daughter died? What would happen to Becky's three precious little ones—the youngest only six weeks old?

Later that day Bob phoned again to say that neither the CAT scan nor the exploratory surgery had given the physicians anything to go on. Margaret and her husband, Martin, booked a flight for the East Coast immediately.

One of the physicians told Bob to get all the support he could. "It might be a long haul," he had said.

When they arrived, Margaret couldn't believe what she saw. Becky was unconscious and her body so swollen that the skin on her arms was tearing under the strain. Tubes stuck out of her arms, neck, and throat, and machines and monitors surrounded her bed. "But," Margaret said, "for her sake I knew I couldn't fall apart. Becky and Bob needed me. I willed my voice to be steady. I told her I was there and that I loved her."

Margaret knew she had no power to change the situation. She turned to the Lord and focused on his love. When the diagnosis was finally made, it was worse than they had feared. Becky had contracted Type A strep bacterial infection, known as the "flesh-eating" bacteria. By day four in the hospital she took another serious downturn. Death seemed imminent. The doctors suggested that she be transported to Massachusetts General Hospital since they had done everything they could for her in New Hampshire.

"Martin and I were shaken to the core," Margaret said. "Bob and I went to the phone and called everyone we knew for prayer. Then my godly son-in-law took my hands in his. 'We've got to let her go,' he said, 'and release her to God's will.'"

"I wish I could say I felt his peace instantly," Margaret told me, "but I can't. I did feel his presence, though, and I calmed down."

During the helicopter flight, Becky went into acute respiratory distress. Both lungs collapsed, and she turned blue. After she was rushed into the hospital, a Brazilian doctor on staff tried a new approach. He increased the oxygen level to inflate her lungs and then drained off the fluid. She came through. God had answered the many prayers offered on her behalf.

Days after this miraculous turn for the better, however, Becky contracted pneumonia. Suppressors were used to keep her vital organs stabilized, but the result was a loss of oxygen to her fingers and toes. "We stood by," said Margaret, "helpless to do anything to stop the fingers on her right hand from turning black, then stiffen and harden."

Finally the day came when the respirator tube was removed and Becky could talk in a hushed whisper. Twelve days had passed since her admittance into the hospital. She looked up and said, "Mom, I love you! You're the best mother in the whole world. I'm sorry I never told you before."

Margaret was stunned. She had waited a long time to hear those words. She started to cry. God was not only healing her daughter, but he was healing their relationship as well. There Margaret was, on the other side of the country in a sterile hospital room where her daughter had nearly died, feeling more joyful than ever!

Still, there was more to endure. Becky's left hand and the toes on both feet recovered their healthy glow. But the fingers on her right hand never returned to normal. A portion of each one had to be amputated.

"We understood that God sometimes leaves a

reminder of the miracles he performs," said Margaret. "In time, Becky will be able to regain the use of her hand for most things." But Margaret did not focus on the losses. Neither did Bob or Martin. God had pulled Becky through. She would go home and take up her life with her husband and children again, grateful to be alive.

Margaret discovered, as each of us can, that when we are weak, God is strong. And *never* will he withhold his love or his joy from those who call upon his name.

WORDS TO REFLECT ON

I will be glad and rejoice in your love,
    for you saw my affliction
    and knew the anguish of my soul.

PSALM 31:7

God is our refuge and strength,
    an ever-present help in trouble.
Therefore we will not fear, though the earth give way
    and the mountains fall into the heart of the sea,
though its waters roar and foam
    and the mountains quake with their surging.

PSALM 46:1-3

If you have any encouragement from being united with Christ,
if any comfort from his love, if any fellowship with the Spirit, if

any tenderness and compassion, then make my joy complete by being like-minded, having the same love, being one in spirit and purpose.

PHILIPPIANS 2:1-2

LOOKING WITHIN, LIVING IT OUT

- In what tough time have you found contentment in the Lord?
- How have you used that experience to encourage others?
- What have you learned about the Lord through such blessings?
- Look for opportunities today to provide your love and support to someone who is going through a tough time.

PRAYER STARTER

Dear Lord, how blessed I feel when I am a gift of light and love to someone who is struggling with pain or loss. Help me to look for these occasions wherever I go today. I want to put aside my self-centered concerns so I can be more alert to those in need. Point to individuals who could use a listening ear, an encouraging word, a loving touch, a personal prayer. Then show me how to squeeze that moment for your glory.

HOLDING ON TO THE JOY

Think about a time when the Lord gave you a joyful experience during a hard time. Describe it and thank him for it.

DAY TWELVE

Listening with a Happy Heart

I don't have a lot of talents," my mother often said, "but people tell me I'm a good friend. I think that's because I listen."

"Mom, if you're a good listener, you don't need a lot of other talents," I assured her. "And you're wrong about the talent part anyway. You're a very gifted woman."

We agreed there's a terminal shortage of good listeners in our society. People like to talk, mostly about themselves, their ideas, their opinions, their problems. And they want someone to listen to them. But if everyone wants to talk, who will listen?

It could be you. Or me. If we choose to make it so. Listening was always a challenge for me. I got into trouble as a kid for talking in class. I had much to say at home around the table. And I loved to hang on the phone with friends until my parents gave me the look that said, "Get off the phone or else…"

Much later in my life I finally realized that listening is an act of intimacy, a selfless act, because it involves being present for another person and allowing him or

her to share heart, mind, and spirit without the inter-
ruption of commentary, advice, or point of view. It can
also be a gift to ourselves. We might learn something of
value from what the other person has to say, though we
rarely think of that ahead of time.

Listening requires little. Yet we often overlook it
when we are considering doing something for ourselves
or for someone else. Perhaps it doesn't seem like enough.
It can't be touched or measured. It may feel too passive,
even boring! But don't underestimate its power. Every
one of us has someone in our lives who would talk to us
more—if we were more willing to listen.

Who are these people in your life? Seek them out.
Make listening a new priority, a gift to the one speaking
as well as to yourself.

I remember a time when I was on the receiving end
of this gift. It came from an unexpected source—my
parents—the very ones who raised their eyebrows at
times when I rambled on and on as a child and then
later as a teen.

One Saturday I stopped by the nursing home where
they lived. Both depended on others to help them with
basic tasks, to drive them to medical appointments, to do
small favors such as potting and watering the flowers on
their terrace, or to help fill their long days by playing a
CD or tape of their favorite music.

That Saturday I hurried into their room all smiles.

As I hugged and greeted them, I began talking a mile a minute (as I'm known to do)! I was on my way home from a family camp where I had spent a week with my oldest daughter, her husband, and their five children. I had one story after another to share with my parents. Their eyes were bright with interest. My father, who rarely smiled (one of the side effects of Parkinson's disease), was actually grinning as I related funny incidents involving his great-grandchildren. Mother squeezed my hand repeatedly, and tears welled in her eyes as I reminisced about similar vacations we had enjoyed as a family when I was growing up.

What great listeners they were. I felt as though I were the Queen of England holding court! The more they responded, the more I talked. Then suddenly I stopped and apologized. "I'm talking your ears off," I said, laughing with embarrassment. "How about if we take a stroll outside? Dad, I'll push you in the wheelchair, and Mom can walk alongside. It's a beautiful sunny day."

My father raised his hand to stop me. "Oh no," he said, "it's such a treat to listen to you." (I don't remember being told that as a child.) "I don't want to waste a moment. Keep talking." So I did, until I had to leave about half an hour later.

Here was a gift so lovely that I cried as I said goodbye. My father, bound to a wheelchair and unable to feed himself, and my mother, no longer able to speak due to a stroke, could *still* squeeze the moments they had with me.

Every talker needs a good listener. My parents were certainly that for me on this special day. I had set out to bring them a few moments of joy and received in return a heart full of happiness.

WORDS TO REFLECT ON

A patient man has great understanding.

PROVERBS 14:29

Godliness with contentment is great gain.

1 TIMOTHY 6:6

Jesus called the crowd to him and said, "Listen and understand."

MATTHEW 15:10

LOOKING WITHIN, LIVING IT OUT

- Who in your life would talk to you more if you listened better? What might help you become a better listener today?
- How could being a caring listener bring joy to yourself and others?
- What would it take to become a more attentive listener to God?

• Today look for ways to listen when you are with someone who needs to talk.

PRAYER STARTER

I feel so good, Lord, when you listen to me. I love to pour
out my thoughts and feelings, my joys and sorrows,
knowing you are always interested and eager to hear
from me. I realize, however, that I'm not as good a listener as I am a talker. I want to improve my listening
skills. Please help me today to experience the joy that is
available when I simply listen, without jumping in with
my opinion or my advice. And help me to know,
whether or not I receive feedback, that my listening—
my active presence—brings joy to you and to others.

HOLDING ON TO THE JOY

Consider the blessing of being with someone who knows
how to listen. Write down what you most appreciate
about people who are good listeners and about God, as
the best listener of all!

DAY THIRTEEN

Holding On to Joy

The kitchen phone rang as Dan was about to slice the ham and fill the water glasses. His family's festive New Year's meal would be ready in minutes. As he reached for the receiver, he glanced at the clock on the table beneath his telephone. It was three o'clock.

"Hello. Happy New Year," he said.

"Hi, Dad. It's Anita."

Dan knew something was wrong the minute he heard her voice. And then came the excuses, the apologies, and the usual list of promises. His adult daughter, once again, wouldn't be with him and her brother for New Year's Day.

"Anger flared within me," said Dan, "and then just as quickly sputtered out. I took a deep breath and said exactly what was on my mind. 'I'm disappointed,' I told her. 'I'm hurt that you waited until the last minute to call. And…I'll miss you. Tom and I will both miss you.'"

Anita knew. She was sorry. But she couldn't work it out. The reasons were familiar. What did it matter which one she used? Dan mused. It was the third year in a row that she'd promised to start the new year with them—

the way it had always been when she was growing up. It was also the third year in a row that she'd broken her promise, usually at the last minute.

"Tom walked into the kitchen with a questioning look as he listened to my side of the conversation," said Dan. "Then he got on the phone and gave his sister a piece of his mind. I took the phone back, wished her a happy New Year again, and said good-bye."

As Dan replaced the receiver, something unexpected and wonderful happened inside him, something he says he has never lost sight of. "I realized that nothing and no one can steal my joy," he said. "Not even my daughter, much as I love her."

What a liberating insight that was for both Dan and his son. "I had been praying for wisdom in relating to my adult children," said Dan. "Things had been a little shaky between us ever since their mother and I were divorced. I wanted to give all this worry to the Lord, but I kept taking it back. Guess I've been a parent too long!"

In the days ahead God continued to show Dan practical ways to walk in joy no matter what the situation or circumstances. "I started taking a daily inventory of my thoughts and actions," he said. "And I prayed for courage to do what was right at work and with Tom and Anita, even when it wasn't popular. Finally, I'm learning to trust God more and myself less. I'm so grateful not to be handling things alone."

Dan said he's also trying to see the good in others. "Mother Teresa once said that she concentrated on only one thing when meeting people for the first time: Christ within them. That helped her keep her perspective. I pray it will help me keep mine too so I can hold on to joy no matter what comes at me."

Ultimately we all discover that no one can make us happy, just as no one can steal our joy. What a relief! We can turn to God confidently, knowing that our happiness does not depend on someone or something outside ourselves. Experiencing joy and holding on to it are between God and us. No one can take it away.

WORDS TO REFLECT ON

Sing joyfully to the LORD, you righteous;
*   it is fitting for the upright to praise him.*

PSALM 33:1

Find rest, O my soul, in God alone;
*   my hope comes from him.*

PSALM 62:5

Now is your time of grief, but I will see you again and you will
rejoice, and no one will take away your joy.

JOHN 16:22

LOOKING WITHIN, LIVING IT OUT

- What recent or past experience threatened your joy?
- What helps you keep it?
- How does your outlook affect those around you?
- Today notice people who try to pull you down. Pray for them. But don't let them rob you of your joy.

PRAYER STARTER

Dearest Lord, thank you for giving me an everlasting joy—the kind that no one can ever take from me. Sometimes I allow myself to be pulled down by the negativity and pessimism of other people, but when I stop and turn within, I know that I have the power, by your grace, to remain peaceful, contented, and joyful no matter what is going on around me.

HOLDING ON TO THE JOY

Fill the space below with your reflections on the source and nature of joy and how it is manifested in your life.

DAY FOURTEEN

Choosing to Love

My friend Kris and I were talking one day about the challenge and sadness we feel watching our parents age and weaken. Her mother had Alzheimer's disease during her final years, and my mother, following a stroke, is unable to speak or read and write. We both agreed that sometimes it's hard to reach out to them at this stage of their lives. We miss the mothers we knew while growing up.

Kris had more to contend with in her folks' last years than most adults with aging parents. She was an only child. Without a sibling to share the burden, almost everything they needed fell to her. They also lived nearby, so Kris was on call to cook for them a few nights a week, to run errands, and to check in each day.

"When Mom and Dad came to our home for dinner, it was difficult," Kris confessed. "I found it hard to work all day and then cook, even for 'family company.' At a time when I felt nearly overwhelmed, two wonderful things happened that took me by surprise.

"My husband began pitching in each night: serving, doing dishes, helping my parents to and from the table.

In fact, when Mom was at her worst, Ron seemed to be at his best! His loving ways and gentle words helped me calm down and see what God was doing through him."

One night when Kris's mother was having a particularly bad time, Kris watched as her husband reached over and patted her mom's hand. "She was crying and complaining and very upset, a real trial to be around," said Kris, "but Ron knew just what to say. He didn't talk her out of the way she was feeling or try to make her understand that she was disturbing everyone. He just said, 'Mom, let's have some ice cream.' He knew it was her favorite dessert. Mom's face lit up—what a change! She seemed to forget her complaints, ready now to receive the treat Ron offered."

But it wasn't only Kris's mother who changed that night. Kris did, as well. "In that moment," she said, "I saw my husband in a new light. I knew then that he would always treat me with the same love and care he extended to my mother, no matter what might happen to me later in life."

Kris said she was surprised at the feeling of joy that spontaneously came over her. And apparently it rippled throughout the room because minutes later, her mother got up from the table, walked over to her own husband, and, in Kris's words, "gave him a love."

"I wish you could have seen my father's reaction," she added, smiling. "This simple gesture took him by complete surprise too. The depth of his appreciation was written all over his face."

All because Ron turned a moment of irritation into a moment of joy by choosing love over negativity.

WORDS TO REFLECT ON

May the words of my mouth and the meditation of my heart
   be pleasing in your sight,
   O LORD, my Rock and my Redeemer.

PSALM 19:14

A cheerful heart is good medicine,
   but a crushed spirit dries up the bones.

PROVERBS 17:22

Love is patient, love is kind. It does not envy, it does not boast, it is not proud. It is not rude, it is not self-seeking, it is not easily angered, it keeps no record of wrongs. Love does not delight in evil but rejoices with the truth. It always protects, always trusts, always hopes, always perseveres.

1 CORINTHIANS 13:4-7

LOOKING WITHIN, LIVING IT OUT

• Which people in your life could especially benefit from a loving response instead of an irritated one?

- When has someone responded to you with love instead of with judgment?
- How does *choosing* to love make a difference in your life?
- Today look at a difficult situation through the lens of love and note the results in your attitude and behavior.

PRAYER STARTER

Dear God, you have given me so much to be joyful about. Everywhere I look I see your hand—at home, at work, in nature, in my family and friends. Despite all this good, I still allow my mind to dwell on the negative: on what I don't have, on what I wish I could do, on how others behave. Today I want to change that. With your help I will choose love over irritation, joy over judgment.

HOLDING ON TO THE JOY

Write an original poem or psalm that reflects what you know and have experienced about the kind of love 1 Corinthians 13 describes.

DAY FIFTEEN

Sharing the Joy

Excuse me," the elderly man said as he tapped me on the shoulder. He had approached me in the hotel lobby during a break from a conference we were both attending. "Are you Karen O'Connor? Someone said you were."

"Yes, I am," I replied.

"The same one who wrote that article for *Reader's Digest*, 'The Best Gift We Can Give'?"

He really had my interest now.

"Yes again," I said, curious as to where his question would lead.

"Well," he said hesitating, "you packed a wallop! I did not like it one bit when you wrote that we owe it to other people to participate in the joyous and the solemn occasions of their lives, that it's almost a duty to be there for them."

I felt my pulse escalate and my joy dribble out like soda from a punctured can. No one had ever confronted me in person about my writing. He even remembered some of the very words I had written. I didn't know what to say.

I began doubting myself. Maybe my editor had been wrong. He was the one who'd encouraged me to write on a topic I felt passionate about. "I want people to finish reading your article, put down the magazine, get up and take action," he'd said, "not merely read your words and then turn the page to the next article." Obviously this man was taking action, but it was against me. I don't think that's what the editor had in mind!

"Sir, I'm sorry my words offended you," I said, trying to hold on to a smile. "But I stand by them. I feel strongly about the importance of people 'being there' for one another. I don't think any of us realizes how much our presence matters." I lowered my voice, hoping to engage his softer side.

Then I stopped, realizing I was defending myself. *You don't owe him or anyone an explanation,* I told myself. *No one can steal your joy unless you allow it. You have the right to your opinion, and he has the right to his.* End of discussion.

"Thanks for letting me know your thoughts," I said lightly, trying to sound polite, "but I need to get back. It's almost time for…"

"Don't you want to hear the rest of my story?" he asked. I noticed a hint of a smile playing on his lips, even though he appeared to be holding it back.

"I'm sure it's very interesting," I said, pulling away, "but right now I'm…"

"It worked!" he called after me. "I didn't like what you wrote, but you were right. I tried what you said, and it worked." His voice boomed now over the dispersing crowd.

I stopped mid-step and turned toward him. "Why don't we walk back to our seats together," I said in a hushed tone, "and you can finish your story as we go."

He laughed. "Got your interest now, don't I?"

"As a matter of fact, yes, you do," I said. I couldn't help smiling.

This curious little man had captured my affection and disarmed me with his off-brand of joy! *What is he up to?* I wondered.

"Well," he said, "I finished reading the article, mulled over your words, and by the time I finished your checklist—you know, be positive about invitations, if possible go out of your way to attend a graduation or a funeral or whatever, and the one about making amends if you can't make it..."

I couldn't believe what I was hearing. He remembered my article better than I did.

"Well, when I finished reading, I got right up, grabbed the phone, and called my brother. He was planning a family reunion in June, and I was invited, of course. Never been to one before. He keeps having 'em every few years, and I keep saying, 'Sorry, can't make it.' I hate those big shindigs. Noise, gossip, kids running everywhere. It's not for me. I live a quiet life. Never been married. Like to do things my way."

I got the picture.

"But something happened after I read that article. Something inside changed," he said in a softer voice. "I got to thinking about my duty. Some of those kids don't even know they have a great-uncle. Never seen me before. And I've never seen them. And my brother— well, he's in his late seventies now. I hadn't seen him in ten years or more."

We were nearing our seats at that point. "I'll get right to it," he said, chuckling. "I told my brother I'd be there, and I meant it. I went just a couple of weeks ago, and it was one of the best things I've ever done."

I noticed tears glistening in his eyes—but just barely, because my eyes were filling up too!

"So you did a good job," he said. "You wrote what you believed in, and it got to me. Thanks. I wish you could have seen those kids. They were all over their great-uncle Bob. That's me! I could feel the joy just bubble up. Never felt so happy in my whole life."

I reached out and put my arms around Bob. He hugged me back. Words weren't necessary. We were both living the article. I had given him something through my writing, and he gave something back through his response. We were "there" for each other in this most unexpected place. And the joy I felt…well, I won't try to explain it!

WORDS TO REFLECT ON

Bring joy to your servant,
for to you, O Lord,
I lift up my soul.

PSALM 86:4

Let us not become weary in doing good, for at the proper time we will reap a harvest if we do not give up. Therefore, as we have opportunity, let us do good to all people, especially to those who belong to the family of believers.

GALATIANS 6:9-10

And let us consider how we may spur one another on toward love and good deeds. Let us not give up meeting together, as some are in the habit of doing, but let us encourage one another—and all the more as you see the Day approaching.

HEBREWS 10:24-25

LOOKING WITHIN, LIVING IT OUT

• What has someone said to you that challenged you to change in some way? What was the result?

- What experience in your life might have been different and better if you had focused on joy instead of giving in to gloom?
- Have you ever disarmed someone with your joyful attitude? What happened?
- Today share your joy with someone else. Build one another up in Christ.

PRAYER STARTER

O God of love and joy, what a pleasure it is when two hearts connect—by surprise, by choice, by decision. However we come together, there is much to be gained. Sometimes I am afraid of what you want to give me through the men and women in my life. Help me today to be open to your gifts of words, prayers, hugs, and help that come through other people. Thank you for opportunities to squeeze the moment with others so we can share your joy.

HOLDING ON TO THE JOY

Jot down an incident where you and someone else shared a moment of joy together. Describe what happened and how it has impacted your life.

DAY SIXTEEN

Reflecting on God's Goodness

The Lord has really blessed us," said Claud, glancing at his wife and oldest daughter, Cheri, as we talked over a meal during my visit to their church in Montgomery, Alabama. "All four of our children have always been a joy to us. And each one knows the Lord Jesus."

I was touched by Claud's sincerity and humility. These were not merely the words of a proud Southern daddy. I could tell they came from his soul. "We didn't do anything to deserve these blessings," Claud continued. "They come from God's gracious hand."

Claud told me how he grew up on gratitude. His mother set the tone. They were a poor family—thirteen children in all. When his father had work, he picked cotton. But often there wasn't any work, and the Walkers went hungry. But no matter. "My mother's theme song her entire life," said Claud, "was the beautiful hymn 'Count Your Blessings.' She gave thanks for everything."

Even in the worst of times Claud said he felt God's hand on his life and he knew the joy of his presence. It was easy to see by the way he treated his wife, Louise, and in his display of affection for his grown children that he hadn't lost his grateful perspective through the years.

The next day I saw Claud again at the church. He handed me a sheet of paper on which was a poem he had written to Cheri when she graduated from high school. What a beautiful example it is of a father's awareness and sensitivity and his willingness to express it.

Never once could we have thought, when you were but
　　a tot,
That raising you could prove to be such pleasure as our lot.
Never were there terrible twos or threes or fours or fives,
But how your smile and rippling laughter brightened up
　　our lives.
Never worried about your soul or made you read the
　　Word,
For you were saved at an early age and loved the things
　　you heard.
Never worried how you'd treat your siblings, old or
　　young,
Nor that you'd find a smile or touch, when things, for
　　them, went wrong.
Never did we lie awake and wonder where you were.
Never did we say, "We really don't trust her."
Never did we have to say, "Be careful how you drive."
Never did you tell us twelve, and then come home at five.
Never once have we felt need to smell your breath for booze.

Never worry of pot or dope or such that you might use.
Never did your teen-age years bring hurt, or pain, or
  crying.
Never once a teacher saying, "She's cheated" or "She's
  lying."
Never saw you with a group which we could not condone.
Never a day that we weren't proud to claim you as
  our own.
Never heard a rebel word or spiteful one from you.
Never once a threat of bad that you would say or do…
So thank you, Cheri, for the NEVERS that we had.
That's why we think you're super girl…from a grateful
  Mom and Dad.[1]

After I read the poem, I realized that in writing this testimony to his daughter, Claud not only did something for someone else, he did something for himself. He took time to reflect on God's blessings and to give thanks. I doubt that Claud would have been able to write such a poem if he hadn't been raised to be alert to life and to thank God for his gifts. Claud's mother had instilled this attitude in her children, and in turn, Claud planted it in his son and daughters.

Linda also experienced the pleasure of God's blessings but in quite a different way. One day while running errands she decided to check out the new department store in town. Linda rummaged through a sale bin and later told me she'd discovered a crushed red velvet hat for only five dollars. She knew just the person to give it to.

"It was perfect for Laura," she said, referring to her twelve-year-old daughter, who is severely disabled as a result of injuries she sustained in a car accident when she was eighteen months old. "Even though she can't converse," added Linda, "she understands her world and usually communicates through tongue signals and smiles."

Linda said she drove home thinking about how beautiful the deep red of the hat would look against Laura's ivory skin and raven-colored hair. "When I showed her the hat, her face brightened," Linda said. Then, suddenly, a most unexpected thing happened.

"Love it!" Laura shouted.

These were the first words her daughter had said in months! "I gave her a hug and placed the hat on her head," said Linda. "I told her that I loved it too. Then I kissed Laura's freckled nose. I held up a mirror and pronounced with joy, 'I think it's the most beautiful hat in the world!' Laura agreed."

How gracious God is to share his presence with us in the small and humble experiences of our lives, as well as in the significant and momentous occasions. He is with us no matter what our circumstances or challenges, and by his grace he allows us to feel his pleasure. As he gives to us, we are able to give to others and to ourselves.

WORDS TO REFLECT ON

In him our hearts rejoice,
for we trust in his holy name.

PSALM 33:21

Give thanks to the LORD, for he is good;
his love endures forever.

1 CHRONICLES 16:34

But thanks be to God, who always leads us in triumphal pro-
cession in Christ and through us spreads everywhere the fra-
grance of the knowledge of him.

2 CORINTHIANS 2:14

LOOKING WITHIN, LIVING IT OUT

- What blessings in your life have caused you to reflect on God's goodness?
- How might praising God every day for his blessings influence the way you live?
- What could you do for someone today that might increase his or her joy?
- Be on the lookout as God provides opportunities to share his blessings with others.

PRAYER STARTER

Dear Lord, you are the giver of all my blessings. What a humbling truth! Help me today to be alert to those around me, especially my loved ones whom I sometimes take for granted, and to look for ways to reflect your goodness in their lives. A warm smile. A firm handshake. Time to walk or talk or pray. A note, a card, a poem, a pretty red hat! All are ways that I can give and receive joy today. Send me out, Lord, and point me in the direction you wish me to go.

HOLDING ON TO THE JOY

Squeeze this moment! Jot down some of your blessings, and write a personal note of praise and thanks to the Lord for his goodness.

[1] Used with permission.

DAY SEVENTEEN

Mourning into Joy

Karen, you may want to stop and visit your parents on your way home. It's not an emergency, but your dad has taken a downturn." This message from my husband was waiting for me at the mule pack station the day I came out of the Sierra Mountains after a week of camping with some women friends.

Suddenly my joyful mood turned somber. I could sense that the end was near. My father had been suffering for a long time, and his decline over the past few months was apparent.

I zipped down the freeway, preoccupied with thoughts of my dad and all the ups and downs our relationship had undergone over the past sixty years. I was filled with memories: of the time he and I sang a duet at a Girl Scout father-daughter dinner…of the week we rode horses together at a dude ranch in Arizona…of the day he walked me down the aisle of our parish church and safely delivered me to my husband…of the time he came to my side when that same husband left me twenty years later.

I also recalled the time he stopped talking to me for

six months because we had some fundamental disagree-
ments about religion. And the time he and I prayed
together for God's forgiveness. Oh, and the precious
time he held his first grandchild and then his first great-
grandchild with the same tenderness that I had known
from him during so many occasions in my life.

I arrived at 1:30 that afternoon, and my sister, June,
and her husband, Harry, rushed in a couple of hours later.
They, too, were summoned home from a trip. We joined
our mother at Dad's bedside and watched as his breathing
became heavier and more ragged. He had slipped into a
coma and could no longer squeeze my hand when I
grasped his. I missed his touch. My father had wonderful,
strong hands, and I was always comforted by them, especially as a child when I was frightened or hurting or sick.

The head nurse entered the room, then told us qui-
etly from the doorway that our father was in the final
hours of his life. It wouldn't be much longer, perhaps a
day or two at the most.

June called her parish priest, a musician friend, and
a few others who had kept a vigil of prayer for our father
during the previous weeks. Sacred music on the violin,
Scripture readings, quiet prayers, and whispered conversation filled the room. All the while my father kept
breathing—in and out, in and out, with greater and
greater difficulty. I could barely stand to watch him
struggle so. I wanted to be there, and at the same time it

was the last thing I wanted to do. I was torn by the conflict I felt.

Dear God, release him, I prayed. *He has waited so long for the touch of your healing hand. I give him back to you, O Lord.*

Suddenly a passage from Scripture came to mind—something about running the race and pressing on for the prize. I couldn't remember the exact wording. Quickly I flipped to the concordance in the back of my Bible, and there I found the key word that took me to Philippians 3:14. In that moment I had an entirely new understanding of what was occurring in front of my eyes. I read the passage aloud: "I press on toward the goal to win the prize for which God has called me heavenward in Christ Jesus."

That was it! Dad was pressing on toward the goal. He was in the final sprint of the race of his life. Of course he couldn't squeeze my hand. Of course he couldn't turn and acknowledge our presence. Of course he was preoccupied with what was happening to him. And of course he was breathing hard and fast. That's what runners do, especially when they are coming down to the finish line. They *press on* toward that goal.

It was a private moment between the Lord and my father, and I had the privilege of observing it. My somber mood began to lift. My resistance gave way to acceptance. Little tendrils of peace—even hints of joy—crept across my heart. I couldn't explain it. My father was about to die and I was feeling happy!

We kissed our mother and father good-night at nine, intending to return at seven the next morning. Then June, Harry, and I drove back to their house, about ten minutes by car from the nursing home. As we walked into the kitchen, the phone rang. It was the nurse.

"Your father is gone," she said. "I went in to check him shortly after you left, and his breathing had stopped."

Reality. Finality. Dad had died.

"He made it!" I wanted to shout. "Hallelujah!" He had crossed the finish line, and now he was in full possession of the prize for which he had run so long and hard.

Though I miss my father very much, I have great peace knowing that he is safe and at rest with the Lord he loved and served all his life. Praise the God who turns our mourning into joy!

WORDS TO REFLECT ON

Those who sow in tears
will reap with songs of joy.
He who goes out weeping,
carrying seed to sow,
will return with songs of joy,
carrying sheaves with him.

PSALM 126:5-6

The ransomed of the LORD will return.

They will enter Zion with singing;

everlasting joy will crown their heads.

Gladness and joy will overtake them,

and sorrow and sighing will flee away.

ISAIAH 51:11

May the God of hope fill you with all joy and peace as you trust in him, so that you may overflow with hope by the power of the Holy Spirit.

ROMANS 15:13

LOOKING WITHIN, LIVING IT OUT

- When and where has God given you joy in especially poignant ways?
- How have you responded to his invitations to depend on him, especially in life-and-death situations?
- In what areas of your life today is God urging you to respond to him with joy?
- Choose one of these scriptures, and consider how it applies to your life right now.

PRAYER STARTER

Father God, I admit there are too many times when I *say* I depend on you, but then when things are difficult, I freeze or wither instead of running to you for counsel and safety. But in my spirit I know that you are the joy of my life! Today I thank and praise you for the many ways you make yourself known to me. Help me, beginning right now, to squeeze each moment for the joy it holds, if only I will respond with a full heart to your love, your mercy, your hope, your compassion.

HOLDING ON TO THE JOY

Compose a poem or psalm describing a time when the Lord filled your heart with joy in the midst of mourning.

DAY EIGHTEEN

Blessing Others

To think of doing something for someone else without acclaim—well, for some folks that's unthinkable. If you must be hugged and loved and thanked and fawned over, then doing for others without expecting something in return is impossible.

But if you want to experience fullness of joy instead of piling up what is merely satisfying, then serving others without waiting around for a pat on the back is the way to go!

Les bought a package of valentines one year to send to his children and grandchildren. He signed his name to each card and filled out the envelopes, then stood in line at the post office waiting to purchase stamps. It was a warm day in Southern California, the line was long, and there were too few clerks.

As Les thumbed through the valentines one last time, he realized he had a spare one. Then he looked up and saw that he was next. Nancy was the clerk who would serve him. He noticed that she looked harried and weary as she scanned the crowd of customers.

Quickly he scribbled her name across the blank enve-
lope, signed his name to the card, and stepped up to buy
stamps. He laid a five-dollar bill on the counter, took his
change, and slid the valentine marked "Nancy" across
the counter. "Have a happy one," he said as he headed
out the door.

"I couldn't resist peeking in the window from the
parking lot," he admitted. "I didn't want her to think I
was coming on to her! After all, I'm happily married.
She seemed to take it as I hoped she would—as a little
acknowledgment from a customer. She was wiping her
eyes when I turned to get into my car."

Les could tell that his gesture had brought Nancy a
bit of joy. What he didn't expect was how joyful *he* felt!
"Such a small thing," he mused, "and such a *big* feeling."

My husband is a lot like Les. In his customer-service
job at Nordstrom in San Diego, he deals with the public
every day. During the horrible fires that ravaged North
County in early 1997, everyone's heart and mind were
filled with the details of this tragic event. Thousands of
homes burned. Precious possessions were lost. Some families were left with nothing more than a shell of a house
and the clothing they were wearing. Nordstrom
responded by offering a 20 percent discount on all mer-
chandise for anyone victimized by the fires.

One woman who had lost everything came into the

store to take advantage of the discount. As Charles rang up this special sale, they talked about her devastating loss. After finishing the transaction, she sat down on a sofa nearby to wait for a friend. Charles then dashed over to the gift department and bought a small box of mints, attached a pretty bow and his business card with a note: "This must be a terribly difficult time in your life. I hope this brings a little sweetness to it."

He walked back to the woman, said good-bye, and while she was distracted in conversation, slipped the box of candy into one of her bags. Charles said he nearly danced back to his post behind the counter! "If I could have kicked up my heels, I would have," he admitted with a twinkle in his eye.

Unknown to him at the time, the story wasn't over. The following day the woman's husband came into the store to buy a suit. He told the salesclerk, Harold, what had occurred between Charles and his wife. "When we opened the bags last night, we noticed the candy," he said. "When we read the note, we sat down and bawled."

Harold, in turn, wrote a note to the store manager, Therese, commending Charles. The next day Therese thanked my husband in person.

What a great example of how one moment in time—like a breeze on a lake—can create a ripple that lasts for hours, perhaps days, even months, all because one man did, on the spot, what his heart led him to do.

Such moments await each one of us if we are alert to life. Imagine seeing an invitation to contribute to a camp scholarship for underprivileged kids and right then, without hesitation, dashing off a check and dropping it in the mail. Imagine the joy that will run through you as you think about some young boy or girl swimming, playing baseball, roasting marshmallows over an open fire later that summer—all because *you* took a moment to invest in him or her.

While shopping at the grocery store, you might suddenly decide to fill an extra basket with bread and sausage and cheese and apples for a single parent in your neighborhood who is struggling to keep enough food on hand. If you really want to be a blessing, drop it off when no one's looking! You'll go home from such an event, filled with joy.

You could buy two tickets to a play, concert, or sports event, and pass them along anonymously. Hold the door for a stranger. Talk with a man or woman whom other people avoid. Empty the dishwasher instead of leaving it for the next person, mow the lawn when no one is home to notice, and hide your good deed in your heart. What you do in secret, your heavenly Father will reward you for in the open.

These are ideas to consider, not things to force or

even plan. Opportunities pop up, like crocuses in early spring. Snatch them. Squeeze them. Then notice the joy…in yourself and in those you bless.

WORDS TO REFLECT ON

Shouts of joy and victory
resound in the tents of the righteous:
"The LORD's right hand has done mighty things!"

PSALM 118:15

In the presence of the LORD your God, you and your families shall eat and shall rejoice in everything you have put your hand to, because the LORD your God has blessed you.

DEUTERONOMY 12:7

I have told you this so that my joy may be in you and that your joy may be complete.

JOHN 15:11

LOOKING WITHIN, LIVING IT OUT

- Has anyone blessed you in secret without taking credit? How did you feel?
- Have you done something kind for another just for the joy of it without expecting anything in return? How did you feel?

- In what area of your life would you like to be more self-less and more joyful?
- Be open today to creating joy for someone else without looking for thanks or praise. Bless as you have been blessed.

PRAYER STARTER

What joy I feel, O Lord, when I live in the moment, able to respond without prodding or pretense, just being the person you've made me to be: a helpmate, a caring friend, a good neighbor, a decent person to those who don't know me. Keep me awake, dear God, alert to the life that pulses around me at every turn. Help me to become more spontaneous in my responses—quick to give, slow to take, happy to do for another regardless of the outcome. I want to focus on pleasing and praising you, not on the pleasure and praise of those around me. Lead me down the path you have set before me, and show me how to squeeze the moments of this day for your glory and for the good of everyone I meet.

HOLDING ON TO THE JOY

Describe in detail one way you have created happiness for someone else without expecting anything in return.

DAY NINETEEN

Enjoying the Gift of Music

During the final stage of my father's illness, a friend of our family brought music back into Dad's world. "I experienced a quiet joy when I played classical music for your father," said Barbara as she shared those events with my sister and me.

She recalled with enthusiasm one time in particular. "While playing a Mozart piece," she said, "your dad seemed to have a quiet but visceral experience of ecstasy. He put one hand to the center of his chest, closed his eyes, then moved his hand down, perhaps indicating that the music was moving through him. There was also a time when we 'hand danced' to show tunes."

Barbara knew the healing power of music from her own experience, and she acquainted me with music's role in healing the sick from as far back as ancient Egyptian times. According to an article she discovered by Edward Podolsky in the July 1933 issue of the former *The Etude* magazine, in 1897 a Dr. Hunter found that music played on a lyre and harp had great value for patients with chronic pain and insomnia. And in 1899

Dr. Herbert Dixon tested the effects of music on his patients and discovered that quick, lively music helped people with slow circulation and low vitality. Soft, soothing music, on the other hand, was a remedy for delirium and night terrors.

I remember meeting a young mother who played Mozart's music each day for her unborn child. She wanted to introduce him to music that would soothe his spirit and energize his developing mind. *What a lovely idea*, I thought. I wish I had known about such things when I was expecting my babies.

Barbara says, "Music inspires feelings of peace and joy. Years ago, my music class at City College motivated me to spend an entire day *actively* listening to Beethoven's music. Life's fire, passion, peace, and sorrow are present in his works.

"My spirit soared," she said, "as I measured the pain and at other times felt the peace. It was an immense sensual experience. The overture, 'Lenore III,' from Beethoven's only opera, *Fidelio*, sent shivers up my spine."

Barbara paused, then added with a wry smile, "I told a friend that listening to Beethoven was the closest thing to making love, without the act itself, that one could experience. She went out immediately and bought all of Beethoven's compositions!"

Music is a gift we can give not only to ourselves or

those we know but to perfect strangers. "One day while running errands with Jimmy in tow," my friend Eva told me, "I let him bring his red-and-yellow tape recorder into the print shop so he could entertain himself while I ran off some copies. After using the machine, I suddenly became aware of how loud Jimmy's Sesame Street sing-along tape might have sounded to the customers and clerks. Just then, Jimmy turned up the volume even higher. He jumped up from the floor and shouted, 'Let's dance!'"

Eva watched in stunned surprise as Jimmy gyrated in the middle of the print-shop floor, motioning for his mother to join him. "Mommy's busy right now," Eva told her son, feeling embarrassed. Then she turned her head to sneak a peek at the print-shop staff. Were they watching the show? No. All the workers, owner included, were standing at their desks, doing the twist to Jimmy's music! Eva said she laughed out loud. "I was surrounded by joy. I couldn't ignore it."

When you squeeze the moment, as Jimmy did, unexpected joy can bubble up like a spring and spill into the lives of everyone around you. Sometimes all it takes is putting on a silly or soft or soothing tune and calling out, "Let's dance!"

WORDS TO REFLECT ON

Let them praise his name with dancing
and make music to him with tambourine and harp.

PSALM 149:3

Be filled with the Spirit. Speak to one another with psalms,
hymns and spiritual songs. Sing and make music in your heart
to the Lord.

EPHESIANS 5:18-19

Come, let us sing for joy to the LORD;
let us shout aloud to the Rock of our salvation.

PSALM 95:1

LOOKING WITHIN, LIVING IT OUT

- What kind of music nurtures joy in your life?
- What new musical expression would you like to experience?
- How could you share the gift of music with someone who might need it?
- Today play a favorite tape or CD, or play your own instrument. Praise God for the sound of music.

PRAYER STARTER

Lord, through the generations your people have danced and sung and played musical instruments to glorify you and to bring joy to one another. I never want to be so focused on work and duty that I forget these gifts from you. Help me today to participate in some musical expression—whether listening, watching, or performing—that edifies you and brings joy to myself and others. Thank you, God, for such simple and beautiful ways to experience your presence.

HOLDING ON TO THE JOY

How has music brought joy into your life? Describe one of your experiences.

DAY TWENTY

Discovering Joy in Unlikely Places

Julie could hardly wait to board the plane. She had been selected to join a team of college students bound for the Republic of Congo (formerly Zaire) in Central Africa for a short-term summer mission. Their purpose was to meet native Africans and to move from village to village, supporting African Christian leaders in showing a film about the life of Christ, referred to as "the Jesus film."

One evening at dusk as Julie and a teammate set up the camera, an African called her aside and asked her to prepare beef stew for dinner. "I felt myself start to boil inside," she said. "That was the last thing I felt like doing. I was annoyed that he assumed a woman had to do the cooking, because that's not what I came for. I wanted to share Jesus with the people I met, not be stuck in front of a stove.

"But I didn't have a choice. He didn't ask if I'd *like* to fix the stew. He told me to do it!

"Then the most amazing thing occurred," she continued. "As I began peeling carrots and potatoes and cutting up pieces of stew meat, I looked up for a moment, and there in the midst of the lush greenery of this tropical setting, I noticed the village huts, as if for the first time. Out front, mothers walked back and forth, busy with their duties, as children played and shouted and ran down the dirt paths.

"I lingered over the scene for a few more seconds when suddenly the sky turned an intense bright orange—almost red. It was the most stunning sunset I had ever seen. I couldn't stop looking at it. Just moments before I had been so focused on what would gratify me—being part of the film crew—that I almost missed this exquisite gift and the entire point of the trip, which was to serve where I was needed. I turned back to the pot in front of me and finished my cooking.

"And, by the way," Julie added, "it was the best stew I ever ate!"

More than a decade later Julie had another experience of finding joy in an unlikely place. "When I began labor for my fifth home birth," she said, "I anticipated getting through the powerful contractions as best I could, while looking ahead to that glorious moment when my new son or daughter emerged."

During the middle of the night, Julie's contractions grew steady and stronger. Soon they became intense, and she geared up for what she knew lay ahead. "I climbed into our small bathtub, and for a while the warm water eased my discomfort. But soon I realized I was heading into the hard part. I called my husband, Jon, my "coach." When he walked into the bathroom, I asked him if he wanted a script of nice things to say to a laboring woman. But he appeared to have written his own script. 'Don't forget to breathe while you get up and make me a sandwich,' he quipped.

"I started laughing and couldn't stop. There, in the toughest part of my labor, with contractions coming one on top of another, Jon cracked jokes, and I cracked up! We were having a private party!"

Julie's midwife knocked on the bathroom door. "Are you still in labor in there?" she asked. "All I hear is laughter."

Within an hour Caitrin Grace joined their family. Julie says, "I will always remember this birth for my 'laughing labor'—moments of intimate joy with my husband during some of the hardest work of my life."

WORDS TO REFLECT ON

From the LORD comes deliverance.

PSALM 3:8

All the days of the oppressed are wretched,
but the cheerful heart has a continual feast.

PROVERBS 15:15

The wisdom that comes from heaven is first of all pure; then peace-loving, considerate, submissive, full of mercy and good fruit, impartial and sincere.

JAMES 3:17

LOOKING WITHIN, LIVING IT OUT

- What happy experience have you encountered in an unlikely place?
- What can you do today to nurture your sense of humor?
- Who in your life could benefit from some humor and cheerfulness during a serious or scary situation?
- Be open today to opportunities to squeeze the moment in unlikely places.

PRAYER STARTER

O God, you do not want me to miss any of the gifts you have for me. You reveal yourself in unlikely ways and places. When I stand in line at the supermarket, there you are in the smile of the cashier. When I pass the homeless man looking for change, there you are, reminding me to give. When I organize my garage, polish my car, chauffeur the kids, or preside over a meeting at work, I feel the joy of your presence as you reassure me with love, encouragement, humor, and guidance.

HOLDING ON TO THE JOY

Describe one way the Lord has given you joy in an unlikely way or place. How did that experience impact you?

DAY TWENTY-ONE

Delighting in Creation

Over here, Magah," my granddaughter shouted. "Look at all these pretty ones." I moved down the beach to where Johannah was sitting. Her cup was already half-full of beautiful seashells. She spread them out for me to see. "Can I keep them?" she asked.

"Of course," I replied. "Let's clean them up. Then you'll have some beautiful souvenirs to remind you of our day together."

We washed each one, noticing how the pink and yellow and pearl-colored flecks danced in the sunlight as we rinsed away the grit. I stood up, brushed the sand from my legs and hands, and took a deep breath. I couldn't imagine anything more wonderful than that moment with Johannah on the beach. "God, your creation is so awesome. You are so good to me," I said as my eyes teared.

Months later I lay under a blanket of stars with Johannah's brother, Noah. We had gone to the Mojave Desert for a youth campout. That night just before falling asleep we held hands across our sleeping bags and thanked God for a wonderful day of hiking and rock scrambling.

Then in a sweet whisper, Noah spoke for both of us without even realizing it. "Magah, don't you wish we could stay here forever? It's so peaceful. When I'm home, I get sick of bikes and computers and toys. They break and get old. But I'd never get tired of this. Look at the stars! And I could climb those hills every day and not get bored. And, Magah?" he asked, raising his voice a little. "I love the quiet, don't you?"

Just writing about this now stirs my memory and my tears. Nature does that to you, and so do little boys! God was there—everywhere we went. And it was so gratifying to know that a grandchild of mine could feel the joy of the Lord and express it so clearly. For many years I missed such moments. Today I squeeze every one of them!

I live near the ocean and love walking along the shore. I also enjoy hiking in the mountains. But you don't have to do either one of these to take delight in God's creation. You can go to a neighborhood park or your own backyard with lawn chair in hand, a sack lunch, a nurturing book, and a willing heart. Read and think, look and listen, pray and consider. Watch for the Lord's loving hand, so evident in the delicate flowers, the flitting birds, the grass shoots pushing through the soil, the bushes and trees and shrubs and vines—all expressions of God's benevolence.

It takes so little to nurture yourself and others in this special way. God has already provided the setting and the "props." All you have to do is show up and enjoy!

WORDS TO REFLECT ON

He split the rocks in the desert
    and gave them water as abundant as the seas;
he brought streams out of a rocky crag
    and made water flow down like rivers.

PSALM 78:15-16

You will go out in joy
    and be led forth in peace;
the mountains and hills
    will burst into song before you,
and all the trees of the field
    will clap their hands.

ISAIAH 55:12

O LORD, our Lord,
    how majestic is your name in all the earth!

PSALM 8:9

LOOKING WITHIN, LIVING IT OUT

• When did you last spend a day in nature?

- What part of God's creation brings you the most delight?
- What are some of your favorite flowers? Buy yourself a bouquet today!
- Set aside some time this week to spend a few hours in the mountains, at a neighborhood park, near a lake, in the woods. Invite someone along and share the joy!

PRAYER STARTER

Dear God, how I praise you for your creation: hills alive with colorful flowers, great waterfalls pummeling the rocks below, high peaks jutting through the clouds overhead, grand old trees framing meadows. My spirit sings with joy at the work of your hands. Help me today to notice your presence in every flower, tree, rock, and creature, and so much more. You have made all this for me, and I take delight in your gifts.

HOLDING ON TO THE JOY

Think about the natural beauty where you live. Write down some of the ways you can squeeze the moment and find joy in creation.

DAY TWENTY-TWO

Participating in Another's Joy

My husband and I recently received an unexpected gift from three people we barely knew. It all started during a trip to Colorado Springs for an artists' retreat at the Franciscan Center. While walking the grounds one morning before breakfast, Charles began reminiscing about the two months he and his mother lived in nearby Manitou Springs when he was thirteen.

He pointed in the direction of Pike's Peak and enjoyed telling me about going to the top on the old cog railway, walking through the glorious Garden of the Gods, shopping at quaint boutiques, and cooking together in their cozy cottage atop a steep hill not far from the old railroad station.

"If only I could see it one more time," he said wistfully. "But without a car, it won't work. Wish we had planned ahead. We could have rented a car and stayed an extra day or two. Then…"

I felt his longing, but I didn't feel supportive. My mind was on the retreat, our purpose for the visit. I didn't want to dilute the experience with a side trip down memory lane! I all but told him so.

Charles returned to the topic several times over the next couple of days until I was tired of hearing about it. Exasperated, I finally asked, "Why not borrow one of the residents' cars? We have a free afternoon on Saturday. Perfect time for you to go."

He was uncomfortable driving in an unfamiliar area, and he didn't want to go alone. So the discussion ended there.

Then Saturday morning our retreat director announced that carpools were forming for a trip to the Garden of the Gods that afternoon. We agreed to go, and Billie, one of the local artists, invited us to ride with her.

Charles knew he might not get to Manitou Springs, but at least he could revisit the Garden. He seemed happy. But as we drove through the Garden and out the other side, we suddenly realized we had gone too far, yet hadn't seen all there was to see. Billie made a quick U-turn, and as she pulled around, I caught sight of a sign: Manitou Springs. Half-Mile. An arrow pointed to a street just ahead and to the right.

As I read it aloud, I could feel Charles tingling with anticipation. "Billie," I called, "could we take a few minutes to drive through Manitou? It's so close," I said, waving my hand out the open window. Then I quickly summarized Charles's experience in this village so many years before.

"No problem," she said cheerfully. I was taken aback by her enthusiastic reception to my spontaneous idea. The other passengers, Scott and Sue, were equally excited. "This will be an adventure," one of them said.

"So, Charles, tell us about when you were here last."

"Let's stop there. What an unusual hotel. Looks like a castle."

"Hey, there's the train station."

I was humbled by the flow of supportive comments and questions.

Everyone was making this experience personal. They appeared to care about the details as much as Charles did. Before long, I caught the fever and couldn't wait for the next place to investigate.

Charles's eyes sparkled as he looked at the familiar spots he hadn't seen in over fifty years. Then it dawned on us that we didn't have our camera.

Once again, "no problem." Sue whipped out her 35-mm and offered to take as many photos as we wanted. She seemed to enjoy playing official photographer. Scott and Billie and Sue all encouraged Charles to pose atop the historic engine in the railway yard. Meanwhile, I ran in to the gift shop, spotted a wonderful poster of the Pike's Peak Railway with the Rocky Mountains in the background, slapped my two dollars on the counter, grabbed the poster, and ran outside. I couldn't wait to surprise Charles with this little remembrance of that rich time long ago.

We clicked a few more photos, then glanced at our watches, realizing we'd miss dinner if we didn't head back to the retreat center immediately.

Charles and I settled into the backseat, rich with new memories and new friends who had taught us, particularly me, a thing or two about the value of participating in someone else's joy.

WORDS TO REFLECT ON

Let the righteous rejoice in the LORD
and take refuge in him;
let all the upright in heart praise him!

PSALM 64:10

And now I have seen with joy how willingly your people who are here have given to you.

1 CHRONICLES 29:17

Love your neighbor as yourself.

MATTHEW 22:39

LOOKING WITHIN, LIVING IT OUT

- How have you felt when you celebrated someone's birthday or graduation or promotion?
- What does it mean to *participate* in another person's joy?
- In the past how have you held back or misjudged the importance of your participation in someone else's happy times? What were the results?
- Consider today how you can include others in your joyful experiences and how you can be a part of theirs.

PRAYER STARTER

O Lord, there have been many occasions when I've backed away from entering other people's joy. I've used excuses to avoid the time and energy it takes to be there for others. Fatigue, lack of interest, busyness—all have kept me from loving others the way you do. I want to change that today. I'm beginning to see what I miss and what other people miss when I'm not there to enjoy their celebrations with them. Each day many opportunities go unnoticed until it's too late. Help me today to be aware of the big and small joyful experiences around me and to enter into them with enthusiasm.

HOLDING ON TO THE JOY

Today take a few moments to jot down some of the joyful experiences you've shared with others. Perhaps you initiated them, or maybe others did. Reflect on these times and how they enriched your life.

DAY TWENTY-THREE

Nourishing Body and Spirit

Whorld I moved to a new house some twenty-five years ago, a neighbor came by carrying a beautiful glass jar filled with a mixture of tea crystals, sugar, and instant, orange-flavored Tang. A pretty ribbon adorned the jar, and on the front she had pasted the recipe for what she dubbed, "Friendship Tea." I was so touched I wept on the spot.

I have forgotten the recipe, but I have not forgotten this nourishing gesture. It was a special moment between us, one I took more to my heart than to my teacup.

I've learned how to nourish myself and others from people who clearly have the gift. The Nelsons, for example, host a come-as-you-are vegetarian potluck supper the first Saturday night of each month. Guests spread the table with food and beverages, eat together, then enjoy an evening of companionship.

Chuck and Marita share intimate spur-of-the-moment dinners with friends and neighbors. "We don't always have an entire evening to spare," says Marita, "but we have enough time to eat together and enjoy some conversation over a simple meal."

Marita says she focuses on the people and the food, not on how presentable her house is. Scented candles, pretty napkins, sparkling glasses, and intimate lighting can make even the simplest fare seem like a feast.

Years ago while visiting my daughter and son-in-law who were living in Morocco, I was introduced to the custom of "afternoon visits." Each day about four o'clock Julie and I would either call on neighbors and friends or open her home to them. No advanced planning was necessary. It was simply the thing to do. If the person we wanted to see wasn't home, we tried again another day. No matter that it might have taken a long bus ride or two to reach our destination!

In Morocco, visiting friends and neighbors is a respected practice, so much a part of the culture that no one questions it or complains that, at times, it is inconvenient. I returned home wishing we had such a ritual in the United States. I missed the cozy chats, the warm sweet tea served in small glass containers trimmed in gold, the welcome break after a long day. But after a few weeks I was back to my routine and didn't think about afternoon visits or hot sugared tea again until sometime later when a friend invited me for lunch for my birthday. She prepared foods that were

new to me: lentil soup, sea vegetables with grated car-
rot, brown rice, and twig tea (yes, twig as in tree)! I
went home nourished by her meal, her friendship, and
her kind gesture.

Today when I think of doing something for someone
else or for myself, I like to choose an activity that will
nourish both body and spirit. Food is a wonderful means
to achieve both. And it doesn't have to take half a day
or more to make it happen.

Vegetable soup and homemade applesauce are two
of my favorite dishes. Both are simple, warming, and festive. During the winter, especially, I prepare meals that
include both. Add steamed rice, hot multigrain bread,
herbed green olives, and hot tea, and you have a nourishing meal in less than an hour. Add good friends and
you've created an afternoon or evening of joy-filled
moments.

In the past I'd never have considered food and
friends around our dining room table to be an important
part of a contented life. Today I know they are essential.

WORDS TO REFLECT ON

May the righteous be glad
and rejoice before God;
may they be happy and joyful.

PSALM 68:3

*I will heal my people and will let them enjoy abundant peace
and security.*

JEREMIAH 33:6

*Each one should use whatever gift he has received to serve oth-
ers, faithfully administering God's grace in its various forms.*

1 PETER 4:10

LOOKING WITHIN, LIVING IT OUT

- In what ways might nourishing yourself and others
  result in unexpected joy?
- What do you most enjoy when you are someone else's
  guest?
- What sounds nourishing to your body and spirit?
  Could you put it into practice today?
- How could you turn an ordinary meal into a festive
  occasion? Pick up the phone right now and invite
  someone to share a joyful mealtime with you and your
  family.

PRAYER STARTER

O Lord, nourishing body and spirit is so much more than
simply offering a meal or a bed to someone in need. You
consider it a gift! You encourage us to use our individual
talents to serve and lift up ourselves and one another.

But I confess that after a long day at work, time with my family, and taking care of personal needs, I am tired. I have little energy left to share. Yet I know I could be enriched by the companionship and conversation of neighbors and friends. Sometimes I simply need a little push in that direction. Provide that today, dear God, so that I can be receptive to the unexpected joy you have reserved for those who serve you by serving others.

HOLDING ON TO THE JOY

List three ways you could nourish your body and spirit. Pick one and write down some ideas for carrying it out.

DAY TWENTY-FOUR

Sharing the Joy of the Lord

You must really enjoy your work," Kathy told the sky-cap as she checked her luggage at the curb. She had arrived at the airport feeling stressed and hassled, but he was so cheerful it was hard not to catch his enthusiasm.

"Oh yes," the man replied. "I love every day I'm alive, and I thank God for it."

"Are you a Christian?" Kathy asked.

His face lit up with a wide grin. He nodded and smiled. "Yes ma'am. That's where I get my joy. I love every day the Lord gives me."

Kathy walked into the airport a different woman. Her stress had disappeared. She whispered a prayer of thanks for this man who had reminded her of what a difference our perspective can make in how we feel.

Standing outside in all kinds of weather and doing routine work day after day would bring out the worst in many individuals. "But he turned service into a gift to everyone he encountered," said Kathy. "The world doesn't expect such an attitude in a society that is overrun with stress and competition, but when someone shares the joy of the Lord, it really stands out."

Kathy was encouraged by observing how this one man honored God through his work. "He brightened my day and helped me change my attitude so I could go on to my speaking engagement encouraged and expectant."

My husband and I had a similar experience. We had spent a week in Dallas at a Christian book convention during one of the worst heat waves in recent history. On the last day we hired a driver with an air-conditioned town car to take us to the airport. It was more expensive than a shuttle bus, but we didn't mind. We were in a hurry, and we were hot!

An hour later, as we pulled into the airport and parked near the sign marked American Airlines, I was suddenly aware of how the heat and stress were affecting everyone around us. Travelers were short-tempered, and airport personnel wiped their brows as they hoisted heavy luggage onto the conveyor belts. Horns honked, and angry bus and taxi drivers swung in and out of small spaces as if they owned the street.

Charles and I jumped out of the car, eager to check our bags and then take refuge in the cool interior of the airport. "Hold on a moment, folks," our driver called, as he pulled our suitcases from the trunk. "I'd like to take a moment to pray for you." He told us he really enjoyed meeting us and discovering that we loved God as much as he did. "Let's ask him to bless your journey." He also asked for our prayers for his new chauffeuring business.

I was so disarmed by this stranger's vulnerability I got teary-eyed! I joined in prayer without another thought to what was going on around us. The three of us huddled together, arms linked, like a coach and two players for the Dallas Cowboys. After a short prayer we hugged, exchanged business cards in case we ever came to Dallas again, and turned to leave.

I looked over my shoulder as our driver walked around to his side of the car. He waved and smiled. "See you in heaven, if not before," I called. A few people stared, but I didn't care. What a send-off!

I walked into the cool airport, grateful for the joy I'd found in this unexpected place from an unexpected source. A man who, less than an hour before, was a total stranger had squeezed the moment so all three of us could share the joy of the Lord.

WORDS TO REFLECT ON

Those who know your name will trust in you,

for you, LORD, have never forsaken those who seek you.

PSALM 9:10

Be devoted to one another in brotherly love. Honor one another above yourselves. Never be lacking in zeal, but keep your spiritual fervor, serving the Lord.

ROMANS 12:10-11

And whatever you do, whether in word or deed, do it all in the name of the Lord Jesus, giving thanks to God the Father through him.

COLOSSIANS 3:17

LOOKING WITHIN, LIVING IT OUT

- How have others encouraged you when you needed it?
- Who in your life could benefit if you stopped long enough to share your spiritual zeal?
- How can you cultivate an attitude of joy as you perform your daily tasks?
- Today be open to opportunities to encourage someone by sharing the joy of the Lord together.

PRAYER STARTER

Sweet Lord, you have given me the ultimate encouragement through forgiveness of my sins and the gift of eternal life with you. What an awesome stand you have taken for me, through your Son, Jesus Christ. Today I draw strength and assurance from your presence, O God, and I want to take your joy into my life and share it with others. Help me to speak words of spiritual encouragement wherever I am—around the dinner table with family or friends, at the office, in a restaurant, at the beach. Let my presence and my conversation honor you and edify everyone I meet today.

HOLDING ON TO THE JOY

Think about a time when you shared the joy of the Lord with another believer in need. How did that experience impact your life?

DAY TWENTY-FIVE

Resting in Joy

Be still, and know that I am God" (Psalm 46:10). This exhortation implies that words, as well as other people, sometimes get in the way of knowing God. Perhaps it's also true that they can get in the way of knowing ourselves. Sometimes the best thing we can do for ourselves is to remain silent.

Why not try it? Take hold of small swatches of time as they appear. Find a few moments each day to be alone without words and without people. Sit under a tree. Take a half-day or a one-day silent retreat. This can take any form you wish—in a church, a garden, a room in your home, a corner of a park.

Practice resting even when other people are around, especially during times of frustration: standing in line, stalled in traffic, or sitting in a waiting room. As we rest in joy, the world cannot so easily disrupt us.

And what fruit the tree of quiet rest bears! We will be healed of the need to speak everything that is on our minds, of the desire to set the record straight, of the compulsion to tell others—even God—what to do and how to behave! We will find purpose in being instead of being a slave to doing. When we allow ourselves to rest, we are more likely to hear God's voice and to receive his joy.

Lynn, a professional singer, speaker, and writer, discovered this truth unexpectedly in the middle of winter. "While driving to a meeting one day," she said, "I felt as void and lifeless as the white sky and frozen roadway in front of me."

Quiet and alone in her car without the blare of radio or audiotapes, Lynn had time and space to ponder and pray, to talk to God about her concerns and fears. She wondered when she would sing again, believing that her twenty-year career was over now that she was the mother of a young child.

She continued driving and thinking, eager to hear from the Lord. Then suddenly, she looked up and noticed telephone wires suspended horizontally across the highway. "They reminded me of a musical staff," she said. "The birds, perched at various levels, looked like small black notes. As I sped by, I sensed they were singing.

"I smiled, realizing in that moment that God would give me a new song one day soon. I drove home to my daughter and husband, confident that I was in the right place. When the time came for a change, he would lead me in the direction I should go. For now, though, I was content and joyful, resting in him."

Richard Foster writes, "Only when we have learned to be truly silent are we enabled to speak the word that is needed when it is needed."[1] Today, when the world presses in on you, at home or at work, step aside. Reclaim silence—even for a few moments. Give yourself the gift of resting in joy. Then when it is time to speak, you will speak the word that is truly needed.

WORDS TO REFLECT ON

Wait for the LORD;
 be strong and take heart
 and wait for the LORD.

PSALM 27:14

Praise be to the LORD, who has given rest to his people Israel just as he promised. Not one word has failed of all the good promises he gave through his servant Moses.

1 KINGS 8:56

Come to me, all you who are weary and burdened, and I will give you rest.

MATTHEW 11:28

LOOKING WITHIN, LIVING IT OUT

• How are silence and joy related?

- What does resting in joy mean to you?
- What would you have to change in order to include more rest in your life?
- Consider, today, a way to increase your contentment in the Lord.

PRAYER STARTER

Dear God, today I want to take time to be with you alone, to feel the joy of your presence without words. I don't want to ask you for anything, tell you anything, worry about anything, plan anything! I simply want to *rest*. When I become distracted, please remind me of this desire. Draw me away from the crowd, and help me to squeeze the moment as I focus my energy and my attention on you.

HOLDING ON TO THE JOY

Take a moment now to rest in the Lord. Then write a brief prayer of praise and thanks for the deep joy that comes when we are silent in his presence.

[1] Richard J. Foster, *Celebration of Discipline* (San Francisco: Harper & Row, 1978), 89.

DAY TWENTY-SIX

Staying the Course

My friend Greg called the other day. He was preparing the proposal for his latest book. "I need to talk," he said. "Got a minute?"

"I'll take one," I said playfully. "What's up?"

"I don't feel like writing this book," he admitted, his voice escalating. "I'm not really interested in telling people how to set up a home office. I don't know how I got myself into this. It sounded like fun when I discussed it with the editor but now..."

His voice trailed off.

I knew what he meant. I was facing a new writing project too and feeling overwhelmed and a bit cranky. It reminded me of the times I took on teaching jobs, helping friends move, writing a column for a tennis-club newsletter, buying a car on my own, and balancing my checkbook—and resisting all the way!

But since I had begun practicing Aunt Grace's precepts, I realized I was more willing to do what needed doing because my life was in better balance than it had been in years. Usually some prayer and an internal pep talk was all it took to get me back on track.

Greg and I set aside the book project for a moment and talked about the "joy" of being freelance writers. Our careers are unpredictable in many ways, and even scary at times, since we report to no one but ourselves. On the other hand, we have freedom and lots of opportunity to be creative.

Before long we had talked ourselves into a good mood! Greg said he felt better. "I'll just do it," he said. "Once I get started, it won't be so bad. I'm bound to learn something. And I have a trip to Florida to look forward to next month."

Sometimes, however, the things that need to be done are more grueling than doing paperwork or car repairs. Some are downright distasteful. They require grit—and grace.

Terrie faced such an experience with her neighbor Jim. When he came down with colon cancer, she decided to visit him regularly and help with shopping. Some days it was just plain hard for Terrie even to enter Jim's apartment. "It was filled with clutter," she said. "And it smelled. He had never straightened or cleaned, and after he became ill, he was unable to clean up after himself. But I put all this aside because he had been a good neighbor, he was alone, and he needed help.

"One afternoon I entered Jim's dark bedroom," she said. "He had reached a turning point in his illness and was losing the fight. I asked him if he was hungry, and he motioned yes, unable to get up. I said I'd bring some dinner before I left for the store, and I volunteered to pick up anything he needed."

When Terrie returned from the market, Jim was eager to pay her for her time as well as for the groceries. Terrie told him she didn't expect to be paid, but he insisted. "He was a strong, self-sufficient person at heart—a giver, not a taker," said Terrie, "so it was hard for him to accept help, especially at such a vulnerable time in his life."

Terrie told him she didn't want to be paid for doing the shopping, but he insisted. So she took the five dollars, said good-bye, and left.

"That was the last time I saw him alive," she said, reflecting on how quickly he went downhill.

A few days before the end, Jim's daughter, who was in from out of town, stopped by Terrie's apartment, carrying a beautiful bouquet of flowers. "My dad wanted you to have these," she said. "We appreciate your help so much."

Terrie said that more than anything, her relationship with Jim showed her what being a good neighbor was all about.

"I learned that sometimes you choose, instinctively, to do some things simply because the need is there and you can meet it. You care for that person in whatever way you can."

WORDS TO REFLECT ON

I was young and now I am old,

yet I have never seen the righteous forsaken

or their children begging bread.

They are always generous and lend freely;

their children will be blessed.

PSALM 37:25-26

He who scattered Israel will gather them

and will watch over his flock like a shepherd....

They will come and shout for joy on the heights of Zion;

they will rejoice in the bounty of the LORD—

the grain, the new wine and the oil,

the young of the flocks and herds.

They will be like a well-watered garden,

and they will sorrow no more.

JEREMIAH 31:10,12

Through Jesus, therefore, let us continually offer to God a sac-
rifice of praise—the fruit of lips that confess his name.

HEBREWS 13:15

LOOKING WITHIN, LIVING IT OUT

• What things in your life do you resist taking care of?
Why?

- What might you do for someone else that you may not feel like doing?
- Have you made a practice of asking God for his grace and guidance as you tackle unfinished projects or difficult relationships?
- Make a list of things in your life that need doing, especially those things you don't like to do. Then choose one and do it.

PRAYER STARTER

Lord God, when I take on tasks that need doing, even when I'm not in the mood, I almost always feel good afterward. Yet I often procrastinate before starting. Remind me that when I lean on your guidance, I can go forward with confidence that you'll be with me all the way. I'm so grateful for the risks I've taken, the goals I've achieved, the experiences I've claimed—all because you have led me out of fear and stagnation. Even my failures have been successes because of the joy you give me when I rely on you.

HOLDING ON TO THE JOY

Describe a time when you did something for yourself or for another that you didn't want to do. What were the results?

DAY TWENTY-SEVEN

Offering Cups of Kindness

Rita came from a large family, and it seemed her mom's sewing basket was never empty—until Aunt Susan arrived for her annual visit. "Then all our mending got caught up," Rita said. Sweaters and shirts got new buttons. Jeans received new patches. Hems were taken up and let down, and waists got taken in and out.

"When I think of Aunt Susan now," Rita mused, "I remember her big lap and her big heart. She and Uncle Will had little money, so they rode the Greyhound bus all the way from Canada to Kansas City each summer. They stayed a whole month. I hated to see them go. They gave us so much attention. And they did all kinds of things around the house for Mom and Dad."

What a legacy Susan and Will left Rita's family. They didn't come to the big city to be taken care of or entertained; they came to visit and to serve. Every day they found a little job that needed doing, and they did it.

For Susan that often meant sitting in a chair with a needle and thread, replacing buttons and zippers and snaps as she talked to her nieces and nephews. For Uncle

Will it meant mowing the lawn, killing dandelions, and putting broken toys back together. He also had plenty of time to read stories and take the baby for a stroll around the block.

Don't we all appreciate it when the right person is right there at the right time? To lift a heavy box into or out of our car, to get us out of a computer jam, to buzz us into our condo when we've forgotten our keys, to take in the mail when we're out of town, to hold the door for us when our hands are full. Moments of spontaneous giving, moments available every day to every one of us.

What small cups of kindness can you offer someone? Could you pitch a tent, type a paper, arrange a bouquet, decorate a cake, fold clothes, read to a toddler, make phone calls, write checks, drive kids to school, deliver a meal, shop for groceries? Or just listen?

Little things *do* mean a lot. Squeeze each moment today. When you have an opportunity to do something for someone else, welcome the joy that comes from offering a cup of kindness in Jesus' name.

WORDS TO REFLECT ON

For even the Son of Man did not come to be served, but to serve, and to give his life as a ransom for many.

MARK 10:45

I tell you the truth, anyone who gives you a cup of water in my name because you belong to Christ will certainly not lose his reward.

MARK 9:41

Freely you have received, freely give.

MATTHEW 10:8

LOOKING WITHIN, LIVING IT OUT

- Who in your life could benefit from your kindness? What could you offer?
- Are you in need of a cup of kindness? What little thing could you do for yourself today that would increase your well-being?
- What is the kindest thing you could do for your loved ones?
- Think about the cups of kindness people have offered you. Give away a few today.

PRAYER STARTER

Lord, you present so many opportunities to me each day to share a cup of kindness. I'm aware of how quickly these moments slip away if I don't wake up to them, pay attention, and act. Help me to set aside my selfish ambitions and preoccupation so I can see the needs around me. Put people in my path who can benefit from my help, my time, my energy. Strengthen me to do your will today. Show me how to squeeze each moment of the joy that is there to give and receive.

HOLDING ON TO THE JOY

Consider today a few of the cups of kindness that people have served you. Jot down your reflections on how they have blessed you.

DAY TWENTY-EIGHT

Preserving Precious Memories

Whenever I look at old photo albums and family scrapbooks, I have my mother to thank for keeping my memories alive. She made a point of pulling together pictures, cards, programs, and ribbons and putting them into a scrapbook for me to enjoy over the years. When she was no longer up to the task, I took over and made her and my father a "heritage" album of their early years.

And I have my father to thank for the adage, "It's the parents' job to create memories for their children." Because of him our family had some of the most wonderful vacations and holidays I can imagine. I remember my excitement when he gathered my sisters and brother around to tell us of his plans for two weeks at the lake, a picnic in the woods, a visit to a museum, a special celebration at Easter or Christmas. Such experiences involved lots of food, photos, fun, and family closeness. I will always be grateful to my father for creating memories I still hold dear.

Preserving precious memories in a keepsake album or book, even when you don't feel like it, is a meaningful way to do something for yourself and for others. Everyone in the family can participate in moving the mountain of photos from a box to a scrapbook. By working and playing together, many happy memories are not only preserved but are relived in conversation.

As you place pictures and memorabilia in your album after a Boy Scout banquet or a Christmas play or a vacation to Lake Geneva or Vacation Bible School, your children may ask questions about similar events in your childhood. What a great springboard for conversation about your early life, your family, your customs and traditions, your experiences as a child.

One of my great pleasures when visiting my in-laws was going through the albums and scrapbooks my mother-in-law had pieced together over the past fifty years. On one page we spotted a couple of uncles standing behind Grandma and Grandpa in their stiff-collared white shirts and knickers. What a find! That led to a long story about the day the photo was taken, the mood they were in, how they felt about wearing their Sunday best on a Saturday!

Another time, my husband discovered his parents' marriage certificate—faded but intact. After his mother died, he retrieved it. We now have it among our treasures from the past, and one day he will pass it on to his children for their books.

Our daughter-in-law, Jeanette, encourages her oldest son, Jordan, to write in the album he's putting together, as well as to add photos and stickers. Photographs, cards and letters, medals and ribbons tell only part of the story. The accompanying personal commentary fills it out, adding texture and emotion to the memory. "My children can sit and look at these scrapbooks for hours," said Jeannette. "And it's their favorite thing to take to school for show and tell."

Children experience a sense of belonging and connectedness through the family scrapbook. They see the chapters of their lives unfold on the page from birth through schooling, church and community experiences, special times with parents and siblings and extended family, and they see their relationship to past generations.

Preserving happy memories in a book is also a beautiful way to connect children to their spiritual history. When I look at pictures of my grandfather, along with notes and cards from him, I am reminded that he was the first person to introduce me to the Bible. I realize today what a strong spiritual impact he had on my life. He didn't preach. He simply lived his faith day to day, attending church services, supporting missions, praying for family and friends, doing small kind things for the children and adults in our neighborhood.

As you and your children work on a scrapbook together, you can show them how your family history displays God's faithfulness. For example, perhaps some of your ancestors emigrated from Europe or other parts of the world to the United States to escape religious persecution. A great-grandfather may have been a minister or Sunday-school teacher. Perhaps someone in your lineage started a church or had a soup kitchen during the Depression or simply lived a good, quiet life that laid down a foundation of faith and integrity that undergirds your family to this day.

By sharing these facts with your children, you are affirming their heritage and deepening their sense of appreciation and belonging. Preserving precious memories in this very tangible way is a gift of yourself to your children.

Like the squares in a patchwork quilt, the photos and keepsakes in your family scrapbook come together to form a covering over your family that will warm each man, woman, and child emotionally and spiritually from one generation to another.

WORDS TO REFLECT ON

Come, my children, listen to me;
  I will teach you the fear of the LORD.

PSALM 34:11

The living, the living—they praise you,
    as I am doing today;
fathers tell their children
    about your faithfulness.

ISAIAH 38:19

*Jesus...said to them, "Let the little children come to me, and
do not hinder them, for the kingdom of God belongs to such as
these. I tell you the truth, anyone who will not receive the
kingdom of God like a little child will never enter it." And he
took the children in his arms, put his hands on them and
blessed them.*

MARK 10:14-16

LOOKING WITHIN, LIVING IT OUT

- Which memory from your childhood brings happiness just thinking about it?
- How do customs and traditions contribute to joy?
- What one thing could you do today to begin preserving family memories and passing on your spiritual heritage?
- Build a new memory with your family this week, and find a concrete way to preserve it.

PRAYER STARTER

Dear God, I take joy in the memories we share as a family. I look forward to the prayer times we have together, the traditions we observe, the songs we sing to praise and worship you, the festive foods and gifts we make for special holidays. I want to preserve the memories of these experiences so they can be carried from one generation to the next. Help me to "squeeze the memories" so my family can enjoy their sweetness.

HOLDING ON TO THE JOY

Consider starting a family journal as a way to preserve precious memories and recount spiritual blessings. Use the space below to describe what you could do to make this a reality.

DAY TWENTY-NINE

Understanding with a New Heart

"One of my friends called," said Joseph, "and the conversation dragged on for forty-five minutes. Pete did all the talking."

Joseph was obviously annoyed. "At one point I nearly fell asleep," he added.

We all know people who impose on us with meaningless phone calls, drop-by visits, protracted conversations in the store, at work, or after a meeting. Perhaps we are guilty of some of this ourselves, though it's hard to imagine!

We might feel like screaming into the phone or behind closed doors, "Hey, when do I get a word in? I have a life too. You're not the only one with problems. This is supposed to be a dialogue. You talk. Then I talk. Get the idea?" But we don't. And the intrusion continues. We might blow up once in a while but then feel guilty, or maybe we simply avoid the person who annoys us.

Joseph got to a point where he made excuses (translation: he lied) in order to cut short conversations with Pete and others like him. "Gotta run." "Someone's at the

door." "We were just on our way out." But those intru-
sive people didn't "get" it. They'd simply call again later
or stop by and go on and on about *their* world, *their* problems, *their* needs.

One night after a particularly boring phone conversation, Joseph crawled into bed and mumbled a prayer in
frustration. "Dear God, please no more of these irksome
conversations. Why do people call me when they only
want to talk about themselves?"

What occurred next took Joseph by surprise.
"Suddenly it became obvious," he said. "These people
are lonely. They have few friends. They need someone to
understand, to be there for them."

If that were true, then what would it really cost him
to extend a little charity, to become more available? He
decided to change his point of view. He tried an experiment. The next time Pete called, Joseph set his own
agenda aside and listened—really listened—to what
Pete was saying. The man needed a friend who would
simply understand. He wasn't looking for advice or help
or a loan! He was elderly, single, and living by himself.
He needed a buddy to talk to.

Joseph realized that *he* could be that person for Pete.
Once he shifted his perspective, he actually looked forward to Pete's calls. And soon Pete was asking Joseph
about his life. They began building a genuine friendship.

Then a most amazing thing happened. "I was in an

auto accident," Joseph said, "and I woke up in the hospital. Who were the first people there for *me*? Pete and others—the very ones I had been so annoyed with. And my wife, who is blind and doesn't drive, was there as well—thanks to Pete who gave her a ride."

These same men continued to visit Joseph while he was in recovery, to drive his wife, Cicily, to and from the hospital twice a day, and to help her care for their pets. "They also arranged for payment of bills and made certain I was getting the right care," added Joseph. "Their help was invaluable. And I was humbled and blessed by the ways God chose to use them in *my* life."

WORDS TO REFLECT ON

Why do you look at the speck of sawdust in your brother's eye and pay no attention to the plank in your own eye?

MATTHEW 7:3

Blessed is the man who finds wisdom,
  the man who gains understanding.

PROVERBS 3:13

You, my brothers, were called to be free. But do not use your freedom to indulge the sinful nature; rather, serve one another in love.

GALATIANS 5:13

Looking Within, Living It Out

- Who would you like to *change* in some way?
- How has your lack of understanding and love interfered with experiencing joy in your relationship?
- What could you do to change your attitude?
- Consider one thing you could do today to show more understanding toward someone you have judged.

Prayer Starter

Dear Lord, you're a God of understanding and compassion. You love all of your people whether we are playful in nature, pushy, peaceful, passive, or perfectionistic. I want to enjoy the differences as well as the similarities between myself and others. I know that I miss so much when I focus on judging people instead of enjoying them. Thank you for showing me your compassion and your understanding. Help me to put it into practice with everyone I encounter today.

Holding On to the Joy

Write down what it means to you to be understood and loved. Then make some notes about how you can offer that to someone else today.

DAY THIRTY

Following God's Leading

During my active ministry, I always started my day with prayer in my study," said Harry, a retired minister. "I liked to sit, palms face up in a gesture of openness. Before closing, I thanked the Lord for all his blessings and then asked him to direct me throughout the day."

Harry was confident that God would lead. Over the years he said he had learned to pray and wait. The Lord never let him down.

One Thursday morning just after Harry finished praying, the word *chicken* came to his mind. "I wondered what that was about," he said, "so I thought, *All right, I'll order chicken and see where it leads.*"

He reached for the phone to call Redman's Barbecue, where he had placed many orders in the past, when suddenly he remembered the chef only barbecued chicken on Tuesdays. But still the urge to order wouldn't go away. Harry said he felt certain God was telling him something, though he wasn't yet sure what it was.

He called Redman's, expecting the usual response,

but the cook surprised him. "As a matter of fact," he said, the chickens came in later than usual so we cooked 'em today!"

Harry drove right over and bought twelve fresh chickens hot off the spit. "The number twelve just popped out of my mouth," he said with a chuckle. "I wasn't sure even then what this was all about." But he had prayed, and he was confident it would lead to something good.

Harry put the chickens in his car and began driving. He didn't have a plan. He didn't even have a clue! But as he drove, he prayed, and he listened for God's direction. He followed the urges he felt to turn onto this street, or into that driveway, sometimes as far away as two miles. "I stopped at whatever house I was drawn to," said Harry, "five in all."

The amazing part of this story is that everyone Harry encountered said they had been praying for food and money.

"At the first house," Harry said, "a man had come home from the hospital recently. He and his wife were in their eighties. She had a heart condition so was unable to cook or shop without help." They were in need of food that very day. The chickens arrived just in time.

"Next I met a woman with three children whose

husband had left the family. She had no food or money. She was really desperate. I left her twenty dollars and two chickens."

At the third house, Harry left chickens for a couple who was ill. The husband was a retired school principal with heart and visual problems, and his wife was suffering with the flu.

When Harry pulled into another driveway and walked up to the front door, he met a man who had lost his job two months before. "I left him a couple of chickens as well as money for food."

The last family needed repairs to their house, and they didn't have enough food, but they had been too proud to ask for help.

"By the time I drove home," said Harry, "I realized I had no more chickens. My wife had the flu, and I had offered to cook dinner that night. When she asked me what we were having, I told her what had happened. 'I planned on barbecue chicken,' I said, 'but they're all gone.'"

Harry opened the pantry, looked around, then turned to Anne and said with a chuckle, "Looks like it's canned stew and crackers for us!"

Later, as they dug into their canned stew—one of the best meals they had shared in a long time—they rejoiced over how God had used Harry to bring unexpected joy to others. Harry had prayed that morning as he did every morning. And God had led him step by step, house by house, through the day.

Words to Reflect On

What other nation is so great as to have their gods near them the way the LORD our God is near us whenever we pray to him?

DEUTERONOMY 4:7

Know that the LORD has set apart the godly for himself; the LORD will hear when I call to him.

PSALM 4:3

If you believe, you will receive whatever you ask for in prayer.

MATTHEW 21:22

Looking Within, Living It Out

• How might a willing spirit make a difference in your prayer life?
• What has God promised to those who pray with faith?
• How has God responded to you when you are willing to serve others without complaining?
• Today consider what God is leading you to do that might require a willing spirit, especially if it's something you are unaccustomed to doing.

PRAYER STARTER

Lord, today I pray with a willing spirit. You have assured me that if I pray, believing, all things will be done according to your will. I embrace that promise. I have seen over and over again that you are faithful to your people when we call on your name. You always direct our steps and lead us in ways that please and glorify you. No matter what occurs in my life, I have the lifeline of prayer directly to you. Thank you for that, dear God.

HOLDING ON TO THE JOY

Spend a few moments in prayer. Then write down what you believe the Lord is directing you to do today.

DAY THIRTY-ONE

Reaching for the Stars

My husband and I were on our way to Kentucky Lake for a family brunch when suddenly Charles pointed out the car window and shouted, "There it is—what's left of the old railroad station. You can see the outline of the platform where Dad and I stood when I left for college."

I caught a glimpse of the remnants as we drove on, suddenly aware of how different it looked from the pencil sketch of the station that hung on the wall of our den, reminding us of a former time when Paducah, Kentucky, was known as a "railroad town."

As we drove and talked of times gone by, I recalled the story Charles had shared with me sometime ago about the morning he stood in front of the railroad station, saying good-bye to his father before going off to college, a day when his father gave him a gift he would never forget.

"I was seventeen and ready to head off into the big world," Charles had told me. "As Dad and I stood on the platform of the little brick railway station, waiting for the 2:37 A.M. train, I was excited—and scared."

They were alone. He had said good-bye to his

mother at home. She stayed behind with his younger brother. "It was one of those still, black nights," Charles recalled. "Fog engulfed the station, and the lights down the line looked like fuzzy glowworms. The only sound was the rid-id-it-tit of the telegraph key. We looked through the station window and saw the operator wearing a green eyeshade, bent over his desk working in the light of a small green lamp."

Then, as if on cue, they heard the train whistling over the river trestle and coming up through the glade some mile and a half down the track. "It was then that Dad turned toward me," said Charles, "and took my hand."

He felt the depth of his father's gaze. He knew he was about to hear something important. "You know, Son," his dad said, "the years pass quickly. Yesterday you were a baby, and today you're a young man. There seem to be so many things we need to talk about, and now there isn't any time left."

"We had always been close," said Charles, "but we hadn't been particularly expressive. We were just deeply fond of each other." Charles said he could tell it was difficult for his father to speak. And it was difficult for Charles to listen.

"Life is full of so much pain and suffering," his dad continued. "I wish I could live that part for you. But that would cheat you of your own quest.

"Son," his dad continued, as he held Charles's hand, "this is a very special time for you. You're going to college, something I was never able to do but always wanted for you. Stand tall, Son, stand on my shoulders. Stand and reach for the stars. Reach for all those things I couldn't reach."

At that moment the train glided into the station, engulfing father and son in a cloud of steam. "When it cleared," Charles said, "we still stood there hand in hand, clinging to one another as best we could. Hugs between men were a bit foreign in those days. I remember telling Dad good-bye. 'Thanks for everything,' I said, my voice cracking with emotion."

Charles squeezed his father's hand a last time, then boarded the train. "I looked down at the lone figure on the platform," Charles continued, "realizing I was leaving my first, best friend behind, going off without him, to do things he only dreamed of...and dreamed of for me."

Suddenly the train moved. Charles waved and so did his father. "The distance between us grew as the train picked up speed. Finally no matter how hard I pressed my face against the window, I could no longer see him. Then the tears came."

Even now, more than half a century later, Charles still gets choked up when he talks about that time. His dad's words echo from the past: "Son, stand tall, stand on my shoulders…reach for the things I couldn't reach."

"Those words have been a guidepost, a beacon in my life," Charles says. "My father's love, integrity, and commitment are what I stand on. They're my foundation. On many a dark night I have leaned on what I saw in him and hoped to find in myself."

Charlie Flowers wasn't a perfect man—but he was the "perfect" father for Charles. In his own way, Charlie encouraged his son to squeeze the moment, to make the most of the opportunities he had ahead of him, to reach for the stars.

WORDS TO REFLECT ON

To the man who pleases him, God gives wisdom, knowledge and happiness.

ECCLESIASTES 2:26

Be on your guard; stand firm in the faith; be men of courage; be strong.

1 CORINTHIANS 16:13

Brothers, I do not consider myself yet to have taken hold of it. But one thing I do: Forgetting what is behind and straining toward what is ahead, I press on toward the goal to win the prize for which God has called me heavenward in Christ Jesus.

All of us who are mature should take such a view of things. And if on some point you think differently, that too God will make clear to you.

PHILIPPIANS 3:13-15

LOOKING WITHIN, LIVING IT OUT

- What legacy has a parent or other respected adult left you?
- What do you consider to be the most inspiring advice you've ever received from an elder?
- How might your words and experience encourage those who come after you?
- Jot down something you could do today that will help shape or influence a young person in your life.

PRAYER STARTER

Dear God, today I want to make a difference in the life of someone else. I know those close to me are watching how I live—the principles I honor, the decisions I make, the behavior I engage in. Lead me, O Lord, and guard my ways. Let me conduct my life so that men and women, boys and girls see you in me and are drawn to live their lives in ways that glorify you.

HOLDING ON TO THE JOY

Consider what it means to "reach for the stars." Then write what comes to mind.

PART THREE

Continuing
the Journey

AFTERWORD

Passing On Your Joy

Perhaps you, like me, have times in your life when you simply want to rest right where you are. You crave time to contemplate a new idea or insight, consider another piece of knowledge, test a new point of view, settle into a new behavior. Certainly times of reflection are essential to our growth as individuals and as men and women of God.

If we get too comfortable, however, we may resist the opportunities that are all around us every day—opportunities to pass on what we know, what we've experienced, what we've learned. If that occurs in your life, I encourage you to resist your resistance! Stop and consider how much you've grown since you've started squeezing the moments of your life. Behold the joy that abounds on every front. Imagine how people around you could change if they knew about and began practicing Aunt Grace's precepts.

Keep on squeezing your moments! And today, move at least one step further. Sharpen your ability to be alert to life so you can pass on to someone else the joy you have. Think of the many people you know who have black-and-white lives when they could be experiencing them in living color! As you share what is occurring within you, they might become aware of how much more joyful their lives could be as well.

Consider taking some more practical steps as you continue squeezing your moments.

At Home

- Continue what you have started in this book. Don't stop after one month! Squeeze the joy out of every moment of your home life from now on.
- Throw a "Squeeze the Moment" party. Invite guests to share at least one joyful moment or event they've experienced during the past week or month. This is a wonderful thing to do as a family. Highlight the party's theme with fresh-squeezed orange juice or lemonade and smiley-face cookies. Plan some games and activities that foster spontaneity and joy.
- Start a tradition in your home: Make a Squeeze the Moment scrapbook. Over the months and years, add pictures, poems, and personal writings that illustrate ways in which Aunt Grace's precepts have helped you create a more joy-filled life.

At Church

- Introduce the idea of squeezing the moment to your adult and children's Sunday-school classes. Dedicate one Sunday each quarter to sharing and fostering the joy of the Lord in some tangible way, such as creating a poster for each classroom or a church banner or an art mural. Invite every man, woman, and child to contribute.

• Plan an all-church potluck supper or summer picnic around the theme of squeezing the moment. Have individuals share their experiences. Plan music, refreshments, even skits that illustrate the theme. Imagine the power of such an event and the impact it could have on people of all ages.

In Your Community

• Consider speaking on the topic of squeezing the moment to senior groups, patients in nursing homes, or service clubs such as Lions and Kiwanis. People everywhere are hungry for more joy in their lives, more wholesome fun, more interaction with others, more expression of honest emotion. Inspire them with the concepts presented in this book.

• Start a discussion group or a book club with joy as the theme. Prepare a reading list of books that help people elevate their thinking and behavior.

"The one who received the seed that fell on good soil is the man who hears the word and understands it. He produces a crop, yielding a hundred, sixty or thirty times what was sown" (Matthew 13:23).

PART FOUR

Personal
Pages

PERSONAL PAGES

Recording Your Joy

I invite you to make the following blank pages your own, to fill them with your thoughts, your individual prayers, your recollections of the moments you have *squeezed* as you've read this book.

Here is a place to make a permanent record of the joyful moments and events you've experienced, to write about them in detail, to preserve them for later reflection, or to share with your loved ones.

Joseph Marmion once wrote, "Joy is the echo of God's life within us."[1] Allow the life of God in you to echo across these pages as you squeeze each moment to the very last drop!

---

[1] Frank S. Mead, ed., *The Encyclopedia of Religious Quotations* (Old Tappan, N.J.: Revell, 1965), 258.